The Little Flowers of St. Francis of Assisi

The Little Flowers of St. Francis of Assisi

BOOK-OF-THE-MONTH CLUB
NEW YORK

Imprimi potest: Celsus R. Wheeler, O. F. M., *Minister Provincial*
Nihil obstat: Bede Babo, O. S. B., *Censor Librorum*
Imprimatur: † James A. McNulty, Bishop of Paterson

—January 14, 1958

CONTENTS

Part I

v

OF THE MOST HOLY STIGMATA OF ST. FRANCIS

Part II: The Life of Brother Juniper

Part III: The Life of Brother Giles

PART I

PART I

IN THE Name of our Lord Jesus Christ crucified, and of His Virgin Mother Mary. In this book are contained certain little Flowers, namely, miracles and devout examples of the glorious poor little one of Christ, St. Francis, and of some of his holy companions, to the praise of Jesus Christ. Amen.

In the first place, let us consider how the glorious St. Francis, in all the acts of his life, was conformed to the life of that Blessed Christ; that as Christ in the beginning of His preaching elected twelve apostles, that they should despise every worldly thing, and follow Him in poverty and in all virtues, so St. Francis for the founding of his Order, elected in the beginning twelve companions, who were to be possessors of nothing but an entire poverty. And as one of the twelve Apostles of Christ, rejected by God for his infidelity, finally strangled himself, so also one of the twelve companions of St. Francis, who was called Brother John della Capella, apostatized, and finally hanged himself in like manner. And this is to the elect a great warning, and a matter of humility and of fear, to cause them to remember that no one is certain to persevere to the end in the grace of God. As the blessed Apostles were wholly marvelous for sanctity and humility, and full of the Holy Ghost, so the blessed companions of St. Francis were men of such great sanctity, that since the time of the Apostles the world had not seen the like; since one of them, like St. Paul, was taken up into the Third Heaven, and this was Brother Giles; another of them, namely, Brother Filippo Longo, was touched on the lips by an angel, like the Prophet Isaias, with a coal of fire; another of them, and this was Brother Silvester, spoke with God, as one friend with

another, after the manner of Moses; another, by the purity
of his soul, flew up to the light of the Divine Wisdom like
the eagle, St. John the Evangelist, and this was the most
humble Brother Bernard, who explained most profoundly Holy
Writ; and another was sanctified by God and canonized in
heaven, whilst still living on earth, and this was Brother
Ruffino, who was a gentleman of Assisi; and so were they
all privileged with remarkable signs of holiness, as will be
declared in the sequel.

II

OF Brother Bernard, first companion of St. Francis

THE first companion of St. Francis was Brother Bernard of Assisi, who was converted in the following manner. While St. Francis was still in the secular habit, although he had already turned his back on the world, going about wholly despised of men, mortified by penance, insomuch that he was looked upon as a fool by many, and as he passed by was driven away with stones and foul abuse, both by his relatives and by others, all of which ill-usage and contumely he bore patiently, as though he were deaf and dumb — Bernard of Assisi, who was one of the richest, and most noble, and most learned in all the town, began wisely to consider within himself the great patience of St. Francis under ill-treatment, and his so exceeding contempt of the world, insomuch that, detested and despised as he was by everybody now for the space of two years, he only appeared the more firm. Then he began thus to think and to say within himself: "It cannot be otherwise, but that this Brother must have great grace from God"; and he invited him one evening to sup with him, and to pass the night. St. Francis accepted the invitation, and took supper with him, and stayed the night also; and then Bernard resolved to make trial of his sanctity. Wherefore he got a bed prepared for him in his own room, in which a lamp was always burning all night. St. Francis, in order to conceal his sanctity, immediately on entering the room threw himself on the bed, and feigned to sleep; and Bernard likewise resolved to lie down, and began to snore loudly, as if in a very deep slumber.

Thereupon St. Francis, believing that Bernard was really asleep, immediately rose from the bed and betook himself to prayer; and raising his eyes and his hands to Heaven with the greatest devotion and fervor, he said, "My God, my God!" So saying, and shedding many tears, he remained until morning, continually repeating "My God, my God!" and nothing more. And this he said contemplating and admiring the excellency of the Divine Majesty, which deigned to stoop down to the world that was perishing, and to provide a remedy for the salvation of his soul, and through him — His poor little Francis — for the salvation of the souls of others. Then, illumined by the Holy Ghost with the spirit of prophecy to foresee the great things that God deigned to do through him and through his Order, and considering his own insufficiency and how little virtue was in himself, he called upon God,

and besought Him that through His goodness and omnip-
otence He would supply help, and perfect that which human
frailty could not do of itself.

Bernard, seeing by the light of the lamp these most devout
acts of St. Francis, and devoutly within himself considering
also the words which he heard him say, was touched and inspired by the Holy Ghost to change his life. In the morning,
therefore, he called St. Francis, and spoke to him thus:
"Brother Francis, I have completely disposed my heart to give
up the world, and to follow thee in what thou shalt command
me." Hearing this, St. Francis rejoiced in spirit, and answered:
"Bernard, that which you speak about is a work so great and
important, that we must ask advice in it from our Lord Jesus
Christ, and beg of Him that it may please Him to show us
His will concerning it, and to teach us how we shall be able
to put it into execution; and therefore let us go together to
the Bishop's house, where there is a good priest, and let us
have Mass said: then we shall remain in prayer until terce,
beseeching God that by our three times opening the missal,
He will show us the way which it pleases Him that we should
choose." Bernard replied that this pleased him very much.

They started, therefore, and went to the Bishop's house,
and after hearing Mass, and remaining in prayer until terce,
the priest, at the request of St. Francis, took the missal, and
having made the sign of the most holy Cross, he opened it
three times, in the name of our Lord Jesus Christ.

At the first opening appeared these words, which our Lord
said to the young man who asked about the way to perfection:
"If thou wilt be perfect, go, sell what thou hast, and give to
the poor, and ... follow Me" (Matt. 19:21). At the second
opening appeared these words, which Christ spoke to the

Apostles when He sent them to preach: "Take nothing for
your journey, neither staff, nor wallet, nor bread, nor money"
(Luke 9:3); wishing by this to teach them that all their de-
pendence should be placed in God, and their whole attention
turned to the teaching of the Holy Gospel. At the third opening of the missal appeared these other words, which Christ
said: "If anyone wishes to come after Me, let him deny himself, and take up his cross, and follow Me" (Mark 8:34).
Then St. Francis said to Bernard: "Behold the advice which
Christ gives; go then and accomplish what you have read;
and blessed be our Lord Jesus Christ, Who has deigned to
show us the way to live in accordance with His Gospel."

Having read this, Bernard departed, and sold all he had
(and he was very rich), and with great joy, he distributed
everything to the sick and to widows and orphans, and
prisoners, and to monasteries, hospices, and pilgrims; and in
all things St. Francis helped him faithfully and wisely. And
one Silvester, seeing that St. Francis distributed, and caused
to be distributed, so much money to the poor, being moved
by avarice, said to St. Francis: "You did not pay me enough
for those stones which you purchased from me for the repairs
of the church; seeing that now you have money, therefore
pay me." Then St. Francis, astonished at his avarice and as
a true observer of the Holy Gospel not wishing to dispute
with him, put his hands into the sack of Bernard, and filled
them with coins, which he placed in the sack of Silvester,
saying that if he wished more, he would give him more.

Silvester, satisfied with this, departed and went home. But
in the evening, reflecting on what he had done through the
day, and blaming himself on account of his avarice, considering
the fervor of Bernard and the sanctity of St. Francis — on

that night and the two following nights he had from God this vision: that from the mouth of St. Francis there issued a golden cross, the top of which touched Heaven, and the arms extended from the East to the West. Touched by this vision he gave away for the love of God all that he possessed, and became a Friar Minor, and lived in the Order in so great holiness and grace, that he spoke with God as one friend does with another, as St. Francis frequently witnessed, and as will be explained more fully later on. Bernard likewise had such great grace from God, that he was frequently rapt in contemplation by the power of God, and St. Francis said of him that he was worthy of all reverence, and that it was he who had founded the Order, because he was the first who had given up the world, and begun the life of evangelical poverty, reserving nothing for himself, but giving everything to the poor of Christ, and placing himself naked in the arms of the Crucified, Whom may we bless forever and ever. Amen.

III

HOW St. Francis, on account of an uncharitable thought which he had concerning Brother Bernard, commanded the said Brother that he should tread three times on his throat and mouth.

ST. FRANCIS, that most devout servant of the Crucified, through the rigor of his penance and by continual weeping, had almost lost his sight, and become nearly blind. It came to pass on one occasion, that he departed from the place where he was, and went to the place where Brother Bernard was, to speak with him about Divine things; and having arrived at the place, he found Brother Bernard in a wood, wholly raised up and united to God in prayer. Then St. Francis, going into the wood, called him: "Come," he said, "and speak with this blind man." And Brother Bernard answered him not, because, he being a man of deep contemplation, his mind was suspended above the earth and raised up to God. Now because this Brother had a singular grace in speaking of God, as St. Francis had often proved, he desired the more to speak with him: therefore after some time, he called him a second and a third time, after the same manner: but neither then did Brother Bernard hear him, nor consequently, did he come to him, or give him any answer. Thereupon St. Francis departed, a little disconsolate, marveling within himself and fretting because Brother Bernard, being called three times, did not come to him.

Therefore departing with this thought, St. Francis, when he had gone a little way, said to his companion: "Wait here for me"; and he went to a solitary place hard by, and prostrated himself in prayer, begging of God that He would reveal to him why Brother Bernard did not answer him. And as he prayed, there came to him a voice from God, which said: "O thou poor miserable little man, why art thou thus troubled? Should a man leave God for a creature? Brother Bernard, when thou calledst him, was communing with Me, and therefore was not able to go to thee, nor to answer thee, seeing that he was so much out of himself that he heard none of thy words." Then St. Francis, having got this answer from God, immediately returned to Brother Bernard, in great grief, to accuse himself humbly of the thoughts which he had had concerning him.

And seeing St. Francis coming towards him, Brother Bernard went to meet him, and threw himself at his feet.

But St. Francis bade him arise, and told him, with great humility, the thought he had had, the trouble in his mind concerning him, and in what manner God had replied to him; and he concluded thus: "I command thee by holy obedience to do that which I shall command thee." Then Brother Bernard, fearing that St. Francis would command him to do something excessive, as was his wont, and wishing, without fault, to escape this obedience, answered him: "I am ready to do this obedience, if thou wilt promise me also to do that which I shall command thee." And St. Francis having promised him, he said: "Now say, Father, what it is that thou wishest me to do." Then St. Francis said to him: "I command thee under holy obedience, that in order to punish my presumption, and the rashness of my heart, when I shall cast myself down on the ground, thou shalt place one foot on my throat, and the other on my mouth, and then pass over me three times, from one side to the other, speaking to me reproachfully and contemptuously, and especially saying to me: 'Lie there, miserable little son of Peter Bernardone, whence comes to thee so much pride, seeing thou art a most vile creature?' "

Hearing this, Brother Bernard, although it went very hard with him to do it, yet, through holy obedience, performed as gently as possible that which St. Francis had commanded. And when he had done so, St. Francis said: "Now command thou me that which thou wouldst have me to do for thee, seeing that I have promised thee obedience." And Brother Bernard said: "I command thee, by holy obedience, that every time we are together thou shalt reprove me for my defects and correct them sharply." At this, St. Francis marveled greatly: inasmuch as Brother Bernard was of such great sanctity that he held him in great reverence, and did not deem him blameworthy in anything; and therefore from that time forward St. Francis took care not to stay much with him, on account of the said obedience, so that no word of correction might come from him toward one whom he knew to be of such great holiness. But when he wanted to see him, or to hear him speak about God, as soon as possible he left him again, and departed; and it was of the greatest edification to see with what charity, and reverence, and humility, the Father St. Francis acted and spoke to Brother Bernard, his first-born son. To the praise and glory of Jesus Christ, and of the poor little one, St. Francis. Amen.

IV

HOW the Angel of God proposed a question to
Brother Elias, and because Brother Elias re-
plied to him haughtily, departed, and went
along the road to San Giacomo, where Brother
Bernard was, and told him this story.

IN THE beginning, at the commencement of the Order,
when there were few Brothers, and the Houses[1] were not
numerous, St. Francis went out of devotion to St. James's
of Galicia,[2] taking with him a few Brothers, among whom
was Brother Bernard. And as they went together along the

---

[1] Franciscan places of abode.
[2] The Shrine of St. James, Compostela, Spain.

road, they found a poor little sick man; and having compassion on him, St. Francis said to Brother Bernard: "My little son, I wish that thou shouldst remain here, to take care of this sick man"; and Brother Bernard, humbly throwing himself on his knees and inclining his head, received the obedience of the holy Father, and remained in that place, whilst St. Francis with the other companions went on to St. James's. Having arrived there, St. Francis remained all the night in prayer, in the Church of St. James; and it was revealed to him by God that he should take possession of many places throughout the world, because his Order would increase, and grow to a great multitude of Brothers; and when this was revealed to him, St. Francis began in his mind to fix upon places in all these countries.

Then St. Francis returned by the same way as he had come, and found Brother Bernard and the sick man with whom he had left him, who was now perfectly healed. Wherefore, in the next year, St. Francis gave permission to Brother Bernard to go to St. James's. And St. Francis returned to the valley of Spoleto, and took up his abode there in a solitary place; himself, and Brother Masseo, and Brother Elias, and some others, all of whom took great care not to disturb, or distract St. Francis at prayer; and this they did for the great reverence they bore him, and because they knew that God revealed great things to him in his prayer.

It happened one day that, St. Francis being in prayer in a wood, a fair youth, dressed as a traveler, came to the door of the Convent, and knocked with such haste and loudness, and for so long a time, that the Brothers wondered greatly at such an unusual knocking. Brother Masseo therefore went to the door, and said: "Whence come you, my little son, for it does not seem you have been here before, seeing you have not knocked according to custom?" The youth replied: "And how must I knock?" Brother Masseo said: "Give three knocks, one after the other, with a pause between each; then wait till the Brother has said a *Pater Noster,* and if in this space he does not come, knock again." The youth replied: "I am in great haste and therefore I knock so loudly because I have to make a journey, and I have come to speak to Brother Francis; but he is now in the wood, in contemplation, and therefore I do not wish to disturb him; but go and tell Brother Elias from me, that I wish to propose a question to him, because I have heard that he is very learned." So brother Masseo went and told Brother Elias to go to the youth; but he was annoyed at it, and did not wish to do so. Therefore Brother Masseo did not know what to do, nor what answer to give; because if he had said that Brother Elias could not come, it would have been a lie, and if he had said that he was so much annoyed, and that he would not come, he was afraid of giving bad example to the youth.

And while the Brother delayed, thinking what to do, the youth knocked again, and a little more persistently; so Brother Masseo returned to the door, and said to the youth: "You have not yet observed my lesson in knocking." The youth replied: "Brother Elias does not wish to come to me; but go and tell Brother Francis that I came to speak to him, but as I do not wish to hinder him from prayer, tell him to send Brother Elias to me." Then Brother Masseo went to Brother Francis, where he was praying in the wood with his face raised towards heaven, and told him the message of the youth, and the reply of Brother Elias. Now this youth was an angel of God in human form. Then St. Francis, without moving from his place or turning his face downwards, said to Brother Masseo: "Go and tell Brother Elias to go immediately, under obedience, to this youth."

Brother Elias, receiving the obedience of St. Francis, went to the door, greatly disturbed, and opened it with a great push and much noise, and said to the youth: "What do you want?" The youth answered: "Take care, Brother, that you be not disturbed, as you appear to be, because anger troubles the soul, and does not allow it to perceive the truth." Brother Elias said again: "Tell me what you want of me." Then the youth said: "I ask thee if it is lawful for observers of the Holy Gospel to eat that which is put before them according to what Christ said to His disciples; and I ask thee again, if it is lawful for any man to lay down aught that is contrary to the liberty of the Gospel?" But Brother Elias answered him haughtily: "I know well, but I do not wish to answer you; go about your business." The youth said: "I could answer that question better than you." Then Brother Elias was angry, and shut the door in a rage, and departed.

Afterwards, he began to think about this question, and to doubt about it within himself, and he could not solve it; because he was Vicar of the Order, and had made a constitution going beyond the Gospel and the Rule of St. Francis, that no Brother should eat meat; so that the said question was aimed expressly against him. Therefore, not knowing how to explain it, and considering the modesty of the youth, and that he said he could answer the question better than himself, he returned to the door, and opened it again, intending to ask the youth about the same question; but he was already gone, because the pride of Brother Elias was unworthy to speak with an angel. This done, St. Francis to whom the whole had been revealed by God, turned towards Brother Elias in the wood, and with a loud voice strongly rebuked him, saying: "Ill done, proud Brother Elias, thou hast driven away the holy angel who came here to teach us. I tell thee, I fear greatly that thy pride will make thee end thy days outside this Order." And so it happened to him afterwards, as St. Francis had told him, for he died outside of the Order.

On the same day and in the same hour that he departed from his place, the angel appeared in the same form to Brother Bernard, who was returning from St. James's, and was by the bank of a great river, and saluted him in his own language, saying: "God give thee peace, O good Brother!" And the good Brother Bernard marveled greatly, and considering the comeliness of the youth, and the language of his country, together with his wishing him peace, and his joyful countenance, he asked him: "Whence comest thou, good youth?" The angel replied: "I come from the place where St. Francis lives, and I went there to speak with him, and I could not, because he was in the wood contemplating things divine, and I did not wish to disturb him. And in that place, Brother Masseo and Brother Giles and Brother Elias live; and Brother Masseo taught me how to knock at the door like the Brothers: but Brother Elias, because he did not wish to answer the question I proposed to him, afterwards repented, and wished to hear me and see me, but he could not."

After these words, the angel said to Brother Bernard: "Wherefore dost thou not cross over?" Brother Bernard replied: "Because I fear the danger, on account of the depth of the water that I see." And the angel said: "Let us cross together and have no fear"; and he took his hand, and in the twinkling of an eye placed him on the other side of the river.

And then Brother Bernard knew that he was an angel of God, and with great reverence and joy, with a loud voice, he said: "O blessed angel of God! tell me, what is thy name?" The angel replied: "Wherefore askest thou my name, which is Marvelous." And having said this, the angel disappeared and left Brother Bernard much consoled; so much so, that he performed the whole journey with great joy, and he took note of the day and the hour that the angel had appeared to him. And arriving at the place where St. Francis was with his companions above-named, he told him the whole story in order, and they knew with certainty that the same angel on that day, and in that hour, had appeared both to them and to him.

V

***HOW** the holy Brother Bernard of Assisi was sent by St. Francis to Bologna, and there founded a House.*

As ST. FRANCIS and his companions were called and elected by God to carry in heart, and to preach in word and in work, the Cross of Christ; and as, both in appearance, by reason of the habit which they wore, and in fact, by reason of their austere life and their acts and conduct, they were crucified men, therefore they desired the more to undergo shame and contumely for the love of Christ, rather than to receive the honors of the world, or the reverence and praises of men. They rejoiced in ill-treatment, they were sad in honors; and so they went through the world, as strangers and pilgrims, taking nothing with them but Christ Crucified. And because they were true branches of the true Vine, they produced great and good fruit of souls, which they gained to God.

It happened in the beginning of the Order, that St. Francis sent Brother Bernard to Bologna, that there, according to the grace that God had given him, he should bear fruit unto God; and Brother Bernard, making the sign of the most holy Cross, through holy obedience set out, and arrived at Bologna. And the children, seeing him in a strange and poor habit, offered him many insults and much ill-treatment, as they would have done to a fool; and Brother Bernard patiently and joyfully bore everything for the love of Christ: and in order to receive the more ill-treatment, he went out purposely to the piazza of the city. There many children and men came about him, and some pulled his hood from behind and some from before; others, in front, threw dust and stones upon him, and others pushed him from side to side; and Brother Bernard, always in the same manner, and with the same patience, and with a joyful countenance, neither got annoyed, nor troubled; and for many days he returned to this place, to undergo the like treatment.

And as patience is a work of perfection and a proof of virtue, a doctor learned in the law, seeing, and considering within himself the great constancy of Brother Bernard, and how he was not disturbed, during so many days, by any contumely and ill-treatment, said within himself: "It is impossible that this should not be a holy man"; and approaching him, he asked him: "Who art thou? and wherefore hast thou come here?" And Brother Bernard for reply put his hand in his breast, and drew out the Rule of St. Francis, and gave it to him to read. And he having read it, and considering its most sublime state of perfection with the greatest astonishment and admiration, turned to his companions, and said: "Verily, this is the highest state of religion I have ever heard of; therefore this man and his companions are the holiest men in the world, and he who ill-treats him commits a very great sin; for he should rather be highly honored, considering that he is a dear friend of God." And he said to Brother Bernard: "If you wish for a house where you can peacefully serve God, I will willingly give it to you, for the salvation of my soul." Brother Bernard replied: "Sir, I believe that our Lord Jesus Christ has inspired you with this thought; and as for your offer, I accept it willingly for the honor of Christ." Then this lawyer, with great joy and love, conducted Brother Bernard to his house; and then he gave over to him the promised dwelling, with all its furniture, fitted up at his own charge; and from that day he became the father and special defender of Brother Bernard and his companions.

And Brother Bernard, by reason of his holy manner of life, began to be much honored by the people, insomuch that blessed did he esteem himself, who could touch him or see him; but he, as a true disciple of Christ and of the humble Francis, fearing lest the honors of the world should hinder the peace and salvation of his soul, departed one day, and returned to St. Francis, and spoke thus: "Father, the House is founded near to the city of Bologna; command the Brothers that they maintain it, and that they stay there; for I have no more profit there, because of the too great honor which is paid to me: for I fear lest I should lose more than I gain." Then St. Francis, hearing all these things, and how God had worked by Brother Bernard, returned thanks to God, who had thus begun and increased the number of the poor little disciples of the Cross. And then he sent forth some of his companions to Bologna and to Lombardy, who founded Houses in various parts.

VI

HOW *St. Francis blessed the holy Brother Bernard,*
and appointed him his Vicar, when the time
came for him to pass away from this life.

BROTHER BERNARD was of so high a degree of sanctity
that St. Francis bore him a great reverence, and constantly
spoke in his praise. It happened one day that, while St.
Francis was devoutly praying, it was revealed to him from
God that Brother Bernard, by the divine permission, should
sustain many and severe combats with the demons, at which
St. Francis, having great compassion for the said Brother
Bernard, whom he loved as his own son, prayed with tears

for many days, entreating God for him, and recommending him to our Lord Jesus Christ, that He might give him the victory over the demon. And as St. Francis prayed thus devoutly one day, God made answer to him: "Francis, fear not, for all the temptations by which this Brother Bernard must be assailed are permitted of God, for the exercise of his virtue and the crowning of his merits; and finally, he shall have the victory over his enemies, for that he is one of the chosen ones of the Kingdom of Heaven." At which answer, St. Francis had the greatest joy, and returned thanks to God, and from that same hour he bore him still greater love and reverence. And this was shown not only in his life but at his death.

For the hour of his death having come, and having, like the holy patriarch Jacob, his devoted sons standing around him, sorrowing and weeping at parting from so loving a father, he asked: "Where is my first-born? Come to me, my son, that my soul may bless thee before I die." Then Brother Bernard said secretly to Brother Elias, who was Vicar of the Order: "Father, go to the right hand of the Saint, that he may bless thee." And Brother Elias, placing himself at his right hand, St. Francis, who had lost his sight through his many tears, placed his right hand on the head of Brother Elias, and said: "This is not the head of my first-born, Brother Bernard." Then Brother Bernard went to him, on his left hand, and St. Francis, placing his arms in the form of the Cross, laid his right hand on the head of Brother Bernard, and his left on that of Brother Elias, and said to Brother Bernard: "God, the Father of our Lord Jesus Christ, bless thee with all spiritual and heavenly blessings, inasmuch as thou art the first-born, chosen in this holy Order, to give the evangelical example, and to follow Christ in evangelical

poverty, seeing that not only didst thou part with all that was
thine, and give with zeal and generosity to the poor, for the
love of Christ, but thou didst offer thyself also to God in
this Order, for a sacrifice of sweetness: — blessed be thou,
therefore, of our Lord Jesus Christ, and of me His poor little
servant, with an eternal blessing, going and coming, waking
and sleeping, living and dying; whosoever doth bless thee shall
be replenished with blessings, and he that would curse thee
shall not go unpunished. Be thou first among thy Brethren,
and to thy commands let all the Brethren be obedient; have
thou license to receive into this Order whom thou wilt, and
let no Brother be lord over thee, but be thou free to God to
come as it shall please thee."

And after the death of St. Francis, the Brothers loved
and reverenced Brother Bernard as a venerable father. And
when he came to die, there came to him many Brothers from
divers parts of the world, amongst whom came that angelic and
divine Brother Giles, who, looking at Brother Bernard with
great joy, said to him: "*Sursum corda*, Brother Bernard,
sursum corda." And Brother Bernard said secretly to one of
the Brothers that they should prepare for Brother Giles
a suitable lodging, wherein he might give himself to heavenly
contemplation; and this was done.

Then Brother Bernard, being come to the last hour of his
life, had himself raised up, and spoke to the Brothers who
stood around him, saying: "Most beloved Brothers, I will not
speak many words to you; but you must consider that the
religious state which has been mine, is still yours, and the
hour which has now come for me, will come for you also:
and I find this within my soul, that for a thousand worlds
equal to this present one, I would not have served any other

master than our Lord Jesus Christ; and for all offenses which I have committed, I accuse myself, and ask pardon of my Savior Jesus, and of you. I beg you, my most dear Brothers, that you continue to love one another." And after these words, and other good instructions, he laid himself down in his bed: and his face grew resplendent, and joyful beyond measure, so that all the Brothers marveled exceedingly, and in this rapture his holy soul, crowned with glory, passed from this present life to the blessed life of the angels.

VII

***HOW** St. Francis passed the Lent on an island in the Lake of Perugia, where he fasted forty days and forty nights.*

T HE true servant of Christ, St. Francis, was in some sense as another Christ, given to the world for the salvation of the people; therefore God the Father willed to make him in many of his actions conformable to the image of His Son, Jesus Christ. This was shown in the venerable company of his twelve companions, and in the admirable mystery of the sacred Stigmata, and in his continuous fast during the holy Lent, which took place in this manner.

Once on a time St. Francis, on the day of the carnival, went to the Lake of Perugia, to the house of one of his disciples, where he was entertained for the night, and there he was inspired by God to pass this Lent on an island in the lake. Wherefore St. Francis prayed his disciple, that for the love of Christ he would carry him across in his little boat to an island in the lake where no one inhabited, and that he would do this on the night of Ash Wednesday, so that no one might know of it. Then the other, for the great love and devotion he bore to St. Francis, solicitous to grant his request, carried him to the said island, and St. Francis took nothing with him but two little loaves.

And when they had arrived at the island, and his friend was about to return to his home, St. Francis earnestly besought him not to reveal to any one what he should do, and not to come again till Holy Thursday. So his friend departed, and St. Francis remained alone; and there being no habitation into which he could retire, he entered into a thicket, where many trees and shrubs had formed a hiding-place, resembling a little hut: and in this shelter he disposed himself to prayer and to the contemplation of heavenly things.

And he remained there the whole of the Lent, without eating or drinking, except the half of one of those little loaves, as was witnessed by his disciple when he returned to him on Holy Thursday, who found, of the two loaves, one entire, and the half of the other. It is believed that St. Francis so refrained from eating out of reverence for the fasting of the blessed Christ, Who fasted forty days and forty nights without taking any material food; and thus with that half loaf he kept from himself the poison of vainglory, and after the example of Christ he fasted forty days and forty nights.

And afterwards, in this spot, where St. Francis had sustained this marvelous abstinence, God granted many miracles through his merits; for which cause men began to build houses there, and to inhabit them; and in a short time there was built a large and prosperous village, and the house for the Brothers, which is still called the House of the Island; and to this day, the men and women of the village have great reverence and devotion for the spot where St. Francis made this Lent.

VIII

***HOW** St. Francis showed to Brother Leo what are the things in which consists perfect joy.*

AS ST. FRANCIS went once on a time from Perugia to St. Mary of the Angels with Brother Leo, in the winter, they suffered greatly from the severity of the cold, and St. Francis called to Brother Leo, who was going on a little in advance: "O Brother Leo, although the Friars Minor in these parts give a great example of sanctity and good edification, write it down and note it well, that this is not perfect joy." And having gone a little further, he called to him the second time: "O Brother Leo, even though the Friars Minor should give sight to the blind, and loose the limbs of the paralyzed, and though they should cast out devils, and give hearing to the deaf, speech to the dumb, and the power of walking to the lame, and although — which is a greater thing than these — they should raise to life those who had been dead four days, write that in all this there is not perfect joy." And going on a little while, he cried aloud: "O Brother Leo, if the Friars Minor knew all languages, and all the sciences, and all the Scriptures; and if they could prophesy, and reveal, not only things in the future, but the secrets of consciences, and of men's souls, write that in all this there is not perfect joy." Going still a little further, St. Francis called aloud again: "O Brother Leo, thou little sheep of God, even though the Friars Minor spoke with the tongues of angels, and knew the courses of the stars, and the virtues of herbs, and though to them were revealed all the treasures of the earth, and that they knew the virtues of birds and of fishes and of all animals, and of men, of trees also, and of stones, and roots and waters, write that not in this is perfect joy." And going yet a little while on the way, St. Francis called aloud: "O Brother Leo, even though the Friars Minor should preach so well, that they should convert all the infidels to the Faith of Christ, write that herein is not perfect joy."

And as he spoke in this manner during two good miles, Brother Leo in great astonishment asked of him, and said: "Father, I pray thee, for God's sake, tell me wherein is perfect joy." And St. Francis replied to him: "When we shall have come to St. Mary of the Angels, soaked as we are with the rain, and frozen with the cold, encrusted with mud, and afflicted with hunger, and shall knock at the door, if the porter should come and ask angrily, 'Who are you?' and we replying: 'We are two of your Brethren;' he should say: 'You speak falsely; you are two good-for-nothings, who go about the world stealing alms from the poor; go your way:' and if he would not open the door to us, but left us without, exposed till night to the snow, and the wind and the torrents of rain, in cold and hunger; then, if we should bear so much abuse and cruelty, and such a dismissal patiently, without disturbance, and without murmuring at him, and should think humbly and charitably that this porter knew us truly, and that God would have him speak against us, O Brother Leo, write that this would be perfect joy. And if we should continue to knock, and he should come out in a rage, and should drive us away as importunate villains, with rudeness and with buffetings, saying: 'Depart from this house, vile thieves; go to the poor-house, for you shall neither eat nor be lodged here'; if we should sustain this with patience, and with joy, and with love, O Brother Leo, write that this would be perfect joy. And if constrained by hunger, and the cold, and the night, we should knock yet again, and beg him with many tears, for the love of God, that he would open to us and let us in, and he should say still more angrily: 'These are importunate rascals, I will pay them well for this as they deserve,' and should come out furiously with a knotted stick, and seize hold of us by our hoods, and throw us to the earth, and roll us in the snow, and beat us all over our bodies; if we should bear all these things patiently and with joy, thinking on the pains of the Blessed Christ, as that which we ought to bear for His love: — O Brother Leo, write that it is in this that there is perfect joy. Finally, hear the conclusion, Brother Leo: above all the graces and gifts of the Holy Spirit, which Christ has given to His friends, is that of conquering oneself, and suffering willingly for the love of Christ all pain, ill-usage and opprobrium, and calamity: because of all the other gifts of God we can glory in none, seeing they are not ours, but God's; as said the Apostle: What hast thou that thou hast not received of God? And if thou hast received it of God, why dost thou glory, as if thou hadst it of thyself? But in the cross of tribulation and affliction we may glory, for these are ours; and therefore, says the Apostle, I will not glory save in the Cross of our Lord Jesus Christ."

IX

HOW St. Francis taught Brother Leo how to answer him, and the Brother could not say anything but the contrary of what St. Francis desired.

ONCE on a time, in the beginning of the Order, St. Francis was lodged with Brother Leo in a place where there were no books to say the Divine Office with. And when the hour came for matins, St. Francis said to Brother Leo: "My beloved, we have no breviary with which to say matins, but in order that we may spend the time in praising God, I will speak, and thou shalt answer as I shall instruct thee, and take heed that thou say not a word other than as I tell thee. I will say thus: 'O Brother Francis, thou hast done so many evils and so many sins in thy time, that thou hast merited hell;' and thou,

Brother Leo, shalt answer: 'Truly, and thou dost merit the deepest hell.' " And Brother Leo, with the simplicity of a little dove, replied: "Willingly, Father; begin, in the name of God."

Then St. Francis began to say: "O Brother Francis, thou hast done so many evils and so many sins in thy time, that thou hast merited hell." And Brother Leo replied: "God will work so much good through thee, that thou shalt go to Paradise." Then said St. Francis: "Say not thus, Brother Leo, but when I shall say: 'Brother Francis, thou hast committed so many iniquities against God, that thou art worthy to be accursed of God,' do thou answer thus: 'Verily thou art worthy to be placed among the accursed.' " And Brother Leo replied: "Willingly, Father."

Again St. Francis, with many tears and sighs, beating his breast, said with a loud voice: "O my Lord, Lord of heaven and earth, I have committed against Thee so many iniquities, and so many grievous sins that I am worthy to be accursed of Thee for them all;" and Brother Leo replied: "O Brother Francis, God will make thee such, that amongst the blessed thou shalt be singularly blessed." And St. Francis, marveling that Brother Leo answered contrariwise to what he had imposed on him, reproved him saying: "Wherefore dost thou not answer as I instructed thee? I command thee, by holy obedience, to answer as I will tell thee. I will speak thus: 'O Brother Francis, thou little wicked one, dost thou think that God will have mercy on thee, knowing that thou hast committed so many sins against the God of mercy and God of all consolation, that thou art not worthy to find mercy?' And thou Brother Leo, Little Sheep, shalt answer: 'By no means art thou worthy to find mercy.' "

But when St. Francis said: "O Brother Francis, thou wicked one," and the rest, Brother Leo answered him: "God the Father, whose mercy is infinitely more than thy sins, will show thee great mercy, and, more than this, will add to thee many graces." At which reply, St. Francis, gently angry and patiently wrath, said to Brother Leo: "And wherefore hast thou presumed to act contrary to obedience, and so many times answered the contrary to what I imposed on thee?" Brother Leo replied humbly and reverently: "God knows, my Father, that each time I had it in my heart to answer as thou hadst commanded me, but God makes me speak as it pleases Him, and not as it pleases me.' At which St. Francis marveled, and said to Brother Leo: "I pray thee from my heart that this time thou wilt answer me as I have told thee." And Brother Leo answered: "I speak in the name of God, for this time I will answer as thou desirest."

And St. Francis said, weeping: "O Brother Francis, thou little wicked one, dost thou think God will have mercy on thee?" Brother Leo replied: "Yea, rather, thou shalt receive great grace from God, and He will exalt thee, and glorify thee to all eternity, because he that humbleth himself shall be exalted, and I cannot say otherwise, for God speaks by my mouth." And in this humble contention, with many tears and much spiritual consolation, they continued till the end of the day.

X

**HOW Brother Masseo mockingly said to St. Francis
that all the world went after him; and St.
Francis replied that this was for the confusion
of the world, and for the glory of God.**

ST. FRANCIS was staying once on a time in the Convent
of the Portiuncula with Brother Masseo of Marignano, a man
of great sanctity, discernment, and grace in speaking of the
things of God, for which reason St. Francis loved him much.
And one day, as St. Francis was returning from his prayers in
the wood, at the entrance to the wood, Brother Masseo met
him, and wishing to test how humble he was, asked in a
mocking manner, saying: "Why after thee? why after thee?
why after thee?" St. Francis replied: "What is it thou

wouldst say?' And Brother Masseo answered: "Say, why is it that all the world comes after thee, and everybody desires to see thee, and to hear thee, and to obey thee? Thou art not a man either comely of person, or of noble birth, or of great science; whence then comes it that all the world runs after thee?"

Hearing this, St. Francis, filled with joy in his spirit, raised his face towards heaven, and remained for a great while with his mind lifted up to God; then, returning to himself, he knelt down, and gave praise and thanks to God; and then, with great fervor of spirit, turning to Brother Masseo, he said: "Wouldst know why after me? wouldst know why after me? why all the world runs after me? This comes to me, because the eyes of the Most High God, which behold in all places both the evil and the good, even those most holy eyes have not seen amongst sinners one more vile, nor more insufficient, nor a greater sinner than I, and therefore to do that wonderful work which He intends to do, He has not found on earth a viler creature than I; and for this cause has He elected me to confound the nobility, and the grandeur, and the strength, and beauty, and wisdom of the world; that all men may know that all virtue and all goodness are of Him, and not of the creature; and that none should glory in His presence; but that he who glories, should glory in the Lord, to Whom is all honor and glory in eternity." Then Brother Masseo at this humble and fervent reply feared within himself, and knew certainly that St. Francis was grounded in humility.

*HOW St. Francis made Brother Masseo turn round
and round, and then went on to Siena.*

ST. FRANCIS was going along the road one day with
Brother Masseo, and the said Brother Masseo had gone on
a little in front, and coming to where three ways met, by
which one might go either to Florence, to Siena, or to Arezzo,
Brother Masseo said: "Father, by which of these ways are we
to go?" And St. Francis answered: "By whichever God wills."
Said Brother Masseo: "And how are we to know the will of
God?" St. Francis replied: "By the sign which I shall show
thee; and I command thee, by the merit of holy obedience,
that thou stand on thy feet, in the place where these three
ways meet, and turn round and round as children do, and
cease not to turn unless I tell thee."

Then Brother Masseo began to turn round and round, and did it so often that, through giddiness of the head, which is caused by continual turning, he fell several times to the ground; but as St. Francis did not tell him to stop, willing to obey faithfully, he rose again each time. At last, when he was turning very rapidly, St. Francis said: "Stand still and do not move." And he did so. And St. Francis asked him: "Which way is thy face?" Said Brother Masseo: "Toward Siena." Then said St. Francis: "This is the way God would have us go."

Now, as they went along the way, Brother Masseo wondered that St. Francis had made him behave as the children do, before the seculars who were passing by; but out of reverence for the holy Father, he did not venture to say anything. And they having come now to Siena, as soon as the people of the city heard of the arrival of the Saint, they went to meet him, and, out of devotion, they carried him and his companion straight to the Bishop's house, in such wise that they did not touch the ground with their feet. At that time all the men of Siena were at strife with each other, and two of them had been killed; but St. Francis having come to them, he preached to them with so great devotion and sanctity, that he brought them all to peace, and to great unity and concord one with another. For this cause, the Bishop of Siena, hearing of the holy work which St. Francis had done, invited him to his house, and received him with great honor, both that day and the night following.

And the next morning, St. Francis the truly humble, who in all his works sought nothing but the glory of God, rose early with his companion, and departed, without taking leave of the Bishop. For which cause Brother Masseo murmured within himself, as he went along the way, saying: "What is this that this good man has done? He made me act as a child, and to the Bishop, who did him so much honor, he said not so much as a word, nor returned him thanks;" and it seemed to Brother Masseo that St. Francis had behaved himself indiscreetly in this. But having, by the Divine inspiration, returned to himself, he reproved himself in his heart, and said: "Thou art too proud, who dost judge the work of God, and art worthy of hell for thy indiscreet pride, for indeed Brother Francis did yesterday so holy a work, that if an angel of God had done it, it had not been more marvelous; therefore if he bade thee throw stones, thou oughtest to do so, and to obey; for what he did on this road came from the divine inspiration, as was shown by the good ending that followed it; because, had he not pacified these fierce people who strove with each other, not only would many more of them have suffered the death of the body, as had already begun to be the case, but many souls would have been dragged to hell by the devil, and therefore art thou most foolish and proud who murmurest at what manifestly proceeds from the will of God."

And all this, which Brother Masseo said within his own heart, going on in front, was revealed by God to St. Francis; and presently, approaching him, St. Francis said: "Those things which thou thinkest now, hold fast, for they are good and useful, and inspired by God; but thy first murmuring was blind, and proud, and vain, and was put into thy heart by the devil." Then Brother Masseo saw clearly that St. Francis knew the secrets of his heart, and understood certainly that the holy Father was directed by the Divine Wisdom in all that he did.

XII

HOW St. Francis imposed on Brother Masseo the
   office of the door, and of the kitchen, and of
   the almsgiving: and afterwards, at the prayers
   of the others, released him.

St. FRANCIS desired to humble Brother Masseo, in order
that the many graces which God had given him might not lift
him up with vainglory, but that, by virtue of his humility, he
might grow in them from virtue to virtue. And as he was
dwelling in a solitary place with his first companions, men of
true sanctity, of whom Brother Masseo was one, he said
one day to the said Brother Masseo, before all the company:
"See, Brother Masseo, all these thy companions have the gifts
of contemplation and of prayer, but thou hast the gift of

preaching the word of God, and of satisfying the people: and therefore I will, in order that these others may give themselves to contemplation, that thou shouldst perform the office of the door, and of the kitchen, and of the almsgiving; and that when the other Brothers eat, thou shouldst eat beside the door of the house; so that whoever comes to the house, when they knock, thou shouldst satisfy them with some good words from God, so that none of them need go to any but thee; and this do by the merit of holy obedience."

Then Brother Masseo drew on his hood, and bowed his head, and humbly received and continued in this obedience, by which he fulfilled the office of the door, and of the kitchen, and of the almsgiving. At which his companions, being men illumined of God, began to feel great reproach in their hearts, considering that Brother Masseo was a man of as great or even of greater perfection than they, and that on him was laid all the burden of the house, and not on them. Therefore they were all of one mind, and went together to the holy Father, to pray that it would please him to divide amongst them these offices, inasmuch as their conscience could by no means endure it that Brother Masseo should bear so many labors. Hearing this, St. Francis yielded to their counsel and consented to their will, and having called Brother Masseo, he said to him: "Brother Masseo, thy companions desire to share the offices that I gave to thee, and therefore I desire that these offices should be divided." And Brother Masseo, with great humility and patience, said: "Father, that which thou appointest me, whether the whole or a part, I account it all as from God."

Then St. Francis, seeing the charity of the others, and the humility of Brother Masseo, preached to them a marvelous discourse on holy humility, showing that the greater the gifts and the graces of God, the more humble we ought to be, since without humility no virtue is acceptable to God. And having delivered his discourse, he distributed the offices amongst them with the greatest affection.

XIII

HOW St. Francis and Brother Masseo placed some bread which they had begged on a stone beside a fountain; and St. Francis greatly praised Poverty; and how St. Peter and St. Paul appeared to him.

THE wonderful servant and follower of Christ, St. Francis, in order to conform himself perfectly in all things to Christ — Who, as it is said in the Gospel, sent out His disciples, two and two, to all the cities and places whither He was intending to go — had, after the example of Christ, chosen twelve companions, and sent them forth into the world to preach, two and two. And in order to give them an example of true obedience, he was the first to set forth, after the example of

Christ, Who began to act before He taught. Now, having assigned to the others another part of the world, he himself, with Brother Masseo for companion, took the way which leads towards the land of France.

And coming one day to a certain town, and being very hungry, they went, according to the Rule, to beg bread for the love of God; St. Francis going down one street and Brother Masseo down another. But because St. Francis was a man of mean appearance, and small of stature, and accounted a vile beggar by those who knew him not, he received nothing but a few mouthfuls and crumbs of dry bread; whilst Brother Masseo, being tall and comely in person, had good pieces, and large, and many, given to him, and entire loaves. When they had begged enough, they went together to a place outside the town, where there was a fair fountain, that they might eat; and beside which was also a broad and convenient stone, on which each placed all the alms which he had begged.

And St. Francis, seeing that the pieces of bread which Brother Masseo had were larger and better than his own, had great joy, and spoke thus: "O Brother Masseo, we are not worthy of so great treasure." And as he repeated these words several times, Brother Masseo answered him: "Father, how can this be called treasure, when we are in such poverty, and lack of things of which we have need; we, who have neither cloth, nor knives, nor plates, nor porringer, nor house, nor table, nor manservant, nor maidservant." Then said St. Francis: "And this is what I call a great treasure, that there is nothing here provided by human industry, but everything is provided by Divine Providence, as we may see manifestly in this bread which we have begged, in this stone which serves so beautifully for our table, and in this so clear fountain; and

therefore I desire that we should pray to God, that He should cause holy Poverty, which is a thing so noble that God Himself was made subject to it, to be loved by us with our whole heart."

And when he had said these words, and they had made their prayer, and partaken for bodily refreshment of the pieces of bread, and drunk of the water, they arose, and went on their way to France. And they having come to a church, St. Francis said to his companion, "Let us go into this church and pray." And entering, St. Francis placed himself behind the altar, and betook himself to prayer. And as he prayed, he received from the Divine visitation such excessive fervor, which so vehemently inflamed his soul with the love of holy Poverty, that by the increased color of his face, and the unaccustomed opening of his lips, it seemed as though he were breathing out flames of love. And coming thus, all inflamed, to his companion, he said to him: "Ah! Ah! Ah! Brother Masseo, yield thyself to me." And this he said three times, and the third time, he lifted Brother Masseo by his breath into the air, and threw him from him, to the distance of a long spear, which put Brother Masseo into the greatest astonishment. And afterwards, relating the matter to his companions, he said that during the time he was raised up and thrown forth by the breath which proceeded from St. Francis, he tasted such sweetness in his soul, and such consolation of the Holy Spirit, that in all his life he had never felt the like.

And this done, St. Francis said to him: "My Brother, let us go to St. Peter and St. Paul, and pray them to teach us, and to give us to possess the immeasurable treasure of holy Poverty, inasmuch as it is a treasure so exalted, and so divine, that we are not worthy to possess it in our vile bodies, seeing that this is that celestial virtue by which all earthly and transitory things are trodden under foot, and all impediments are lifted away from the soul, so that she can freely unite herself to the Eternal God. And this is the virtue which makes the soul, while still retained on earth, converse with the angels in heaven, and this it is which accompanied Christ to His Cross, with Christ was buried, with Christ was raised up, with Christ ascended into heaven, which, being given in this life to the souls who are enamored of it, facilitates their flight to heaven, seeing that it guards the arms of true humility and charity. And therefore let us pray the most holy Apostles of Christ, who were perfect lovers of this pearl of the Gospel of Christ, that they will beg for us this grace from our Lord Jesus Christ, that, by His most holy mercy, He would grant us the merit to be true lovers, observers, and humble disciples of this most precious, most lovable, evangelical Poverty."

And thus speaking, they arrived in Rome, and entered the church of St. Peter; and St. Francis placed himself in prayer in a corner of the church, and Brother Masseo in another. And as St. Francis prayed for a long time, with many tears and great devotion, the most holy Apostles Peter and Paul appeared to him in great splendor, and said: "Because thou hast asked and desired to observe that which Christ and the holy Apostles observed, the Lord Jesus Christ has sent us to thee, to announce that thy prayer is heard, and it is granted of God to thee and thy followers to possess perfectly the treasure of most holy Poverty. And further, in His name, we say to thee that whosoever, after thy example, shall follow perfectly after this desire, he shall be secure of the blessedness of life eternal; and thou and all thy followers shall be blessed of God." And having said these words they vanished, leaving St. Francis full of consolation, who, rising from his prayer, returned to his companion, and asked him if God had revealed nothing to him, and he answered him, nothing. Then St. Francis told him how the holy Apostles had appeared to him, and what they had revealed to him. At which both of them, filled with joy, determined to return by the valley of Spoleto, and to abandon the journey into France.

XIV

*AS St. Francis and his Brothers were speaking of
our Divine Lord, He appeared in their midst.*

ST. FRANCIS, in the beginning of his religious life, having
retired with his companions to speak together of Christ; in
the fervor of his spirit he commanded one of them, in the
name of God, to open his mouth, and to speak of God as
the Holy Spirit should inspire him. As soon as the Brother
fulfilled the command, and spoke of God marvelously, St.
Francis imposed silence on him, and gave the same command
to another Brother. This one also obeyed, and spoke of
God with subtle insight, and St. Francis imposed silence on
him also, and commanded a third to speak of God, and he
similarly began to speak so profoundly of the secret things

of God, that St. Francis knew certainly that, like the other two, he spoke by inspiration of the Holy Spirit. And this was proved also by example, and by express sign; for as they were thus speaking, there appeared the Blessed Christ in the midst of them, under the appearance and form of a beautiful youth, and blessed them all, filling them all with so much grace and sweetness, that they were all ravished out of themselves, and lay as though dead, not feeling anything of this world. And then, returning to himself, St. Francis said to them: "My beloved Brothers, render thanks to God, Who has willed, by the mouth of the simple, to reveal the treasures of the Divine Wisdom; because God is He Who opens the mouth of the dumb, and makes the tongue of the simple to speak most wisely."

XV

HOW St. Clare ate with St. Francis and his companion Brothers at St. Mary of the Angels.

WHEN St. Francis was staying at Assisi, he went several times to visit St. Clare, and to give her holy instructions. She had a very great desire to eat with him for once, and prayed him for this many times, but he would not consent to give her this consolation. When his companions had heard of the desire of St. Clare, they said to St. Francis: "Father, this stiffness seems to us, not according to divine charity, seeing Sister Clare is a virgin, which is a thing holy and well pleasing to God — namely, that thou shouldst refuse her in such a little matter as eating with thee; and especially considering that, at thy preaching, she abandoned the riches and pomps of the world. And to say the truth, if she asked thee a greater favor than this, thou oughtest to do it for this thy spiritual plant." Then St. Francis answered: "Does it seem to you that I ought to consent?" and his companions replied: "Father, yes, a right thing it is that thou shouldst grant her this favor and consolation." Then said St. Francis: "Since it seems so to you, it seems so to me also; but that she may be more consoled, I will have her eat with me at St. Mary of the Angels, because she has been so long a time secluded at St. Damian's, that it will give her joy to see the place of the Blessed Mary, where she was shorn and made the Spouse of Jesus Christ; and there we shall eat together in the name of God."

The day appointed therefore having come, St. Clare, with one companion, came out of her convent, and accompanied by the companions of St. Francis, went to St. Mary of the Angels, and saluted devoutly before her altar the Holy Virgin Mary, in the place where her hair had been cut off, and where she had received the veil. Then they led her into the house, until it should be the hour to dine. And meanwhile, St. Francis had the dinner table prepared on the bare ground, as was his custom, and the hour for dinner being come, they seated themselves together, St. Francis and St. Clare, and one of the companions of St. Francis with the companion of St. Clare, and then all the other companions, humbly seating themselves round the table. And at the first dish, St. Francis began to talk of God in a manner so sweet, so admirable, and so sublime, that there descended upon them the abundance of divine grace, and they were all ravished in God.

And as they were thus ravished, with their eyes and their hands raised towards heaven, the men of Assisi, and of Bettona, and of the surrounding country, saw that St. Mary of the Angels, and the whole house, and the wood which led up to the house, were burning brightly, and it seemed as though a great fire filled the church and the house and the whole wood together, so that they ran thither with great haste to extinguish the flames, verily believing that the whole place was on fire. But when they came to the house and found nothing, they entered and found St. Francis and St. Clare, with all their company, sitting round this humble table, and ravished in the contemplation of God. From this they understood with certainty that what they had seen was a divine, and not a material fire, which God had caused miraculously to appear, in order to show and to signify the fire of Divine Love, which inflamed the souls of these holy Brothers and holy Religious; and they departed with great consolation in their hearts, and holy edification.

Then after a long space, St. Francis returned to himself, and St. Clare also, with all the others, and felt well comforted within themselves by their spiritual nourishment, little as they had partaken of the bodily refreshment. And afterwards, this blessed feast being ended, St. Clare, well escorted, returned to St. Damian's; where the sisters seeing her had great joy, for they feared lest St. Francis had sent her to govern some other convent, just as he had sent Sister Agnes, their holy Sister, as Abbess, to govern the convent of Monticelli, at Florence; and since St. Francis had said one time to St. Clare: "Be ready, in case I have need to send thee to another House;" and she, as the daughter of holy Obedience had answered: "Father, I am ready always to go wheresoever thou wilt send me." And therefore the sisters rejoiced greatly, when they saw her again; and St. Clare received from this also much consolation.

XVI

*HOW St. Francis received the counsel of St. Clare,
   and of the holy Brother Silvester, that he
   should preach for the conversion of many;
   and how he founded the Third Order, and
   preached to the birds.*

THE humble servant of Christ, St. Francis, a short time
after his conversion, having already gathered many companions
and received them into the Order, entered into great consideration and great doubt what he should do: whether he should
give himself solely to prayer, or whether he should sometimes
preach: and he desired much to know the will of God in this
matter. And because the holy humility that was in him
suffered him not to presume on himself, nor on his own

prayers, he thought to discover the Divine Will through the prayers of others: and he called Brother Masseo, and spoke thus: "Go to Sister Clare, and tell her from me to pray fervently to God, she and some of her most spiritual daughters, that it may please Him to show which is the best, whether I should give myself to preaching, or solely to prayer; and then go to Brother Silvester, and say the same to him." The same Brother Silvester it was, who, when he was in the secular state, had seen a cross of gold proceeding from the mouth of St. Francis, which went lengthwise as far as heaven, and the arms of which extended to the extremities of the world; and the same Brother Silvester was also of so great devotion and sanctity that many times he spoke with God, and whatsoever he asked of God was granted, and for this cause St. Francis had a great devotion towards him.

Brother Masseo therefore departed, and according to the command of St. Francis, made his embassy first to St. Clare, and afterwards to Brother Silvester, who, as soon as he knew wherefore he had come, immediately betook himself to prayer. And when he had received the Divine answer, he turned to Brother Masseo and spoke thus: "This is what God says: thou shalt tell Brother Francis that God has not called him to this state solely for himself, but that he may gain much fruit in the souls of others, and that many through him may be saved."

Having received this answer, Brother Masseo returned to St. Clare, to know what she had obtained of God; and she replied that she and her companions had received from God the same answer as Brother Silvester. With this reply Brother Masseo returned to St. Francis; and St. Francis received him with the greatest charity, washed his feet, and prepared his repast; and after he had eaten, St. Francis called him into the wood; and kneeling before him, he let down his hood, and stretching out his arms in the form of the Cross, he asked: "What does my Lord Jesus Christ command that I should do?" Brother Masseo answered: "As to Brother Silvester, so to Sister Clare, with her sisters, has Christ answered and revealed: that His will is, that thou shouldst go into the world to preach, because He has not elected thee for thyself alone, but also for the salvation of others." Then St. Francis, having heard this reply and knowing by this, what was the will of Jesus Christ, arose, with great fervor, and said: "Let us go, in the Name of God"; and he took for his companions Brother Masseo and Brother Agnolo, both holy men.

And going by the prompting of the Holy Ghost, without taking thought of the way or the road, he came to a village called Savurniano. And St. Francis began to preach: and first of all he commanded the swallows who were singing that they should keep silence, until he had done preaching; and the swallows obeyed him. And he preached with so much fervor, that all the men and women in that village were minded to go forth, and abandon the village. But St. Francis suffered them not, and said to them: "Do not be in haste, and do not go hence, and I will order that which you must do, for the salvation of your souls"; and then he thought of his Third Order, for the salvation of the whole world. And he left them much comforted, and well-disposed to penance; and he departed thence, and went by Cannaio and Bevagno.

And passing along, in fervor of soul, he lifted up his eyes and saw many trees standing by the way, and filled with a countless multitude of little birds; at which St. Francis wondered, and said to his companions: "Wait a little for me in

the road, and I will go and preach to my sisters the birds."
And he entered into the field, and began to preach to the
birds that were on the ground. And suddenly those that were
in the trees came around him, and together they all remained
silent, so long as it pleased St. Francis to speak; and even
after he had finished they would not depart until he had
given them his blessing. And according as Brother Masseo
afterward related to Brother James of La Massa, St. Francis
went among them and touched them with his cloak, and none
of them moved.

The substance of the sermon was this: "My little sisters,
the birds, you are much beholden to God your Creator, and
in all places you ought to praise Him, because He has given
you liberty to fly about in all places, and has given you double
and triple raiment. Know also, that He preserved your race
in the ark of Noe that your species might not perish. And
again, you are beholden to Him for the element of air, which
He has appointed for you; and for this also, that you neither
sow nor reap, but God feeds you, and gives you the brooks and
fountains for your drink, the mountains and valleys also for
your refuge, and the tall trees wherein to make your nests.
And since you know neither how to sew nor to spin, God
clothes you, you and your young ones. Wherefore your
Creator loves you much, since He has bestowed on you so
many benefits. And therefore beware, my little sisters, of the
sin of ingratitude, and study always to please God."

As St. Francis spoke thus to them, all the multitude of
these birds opened their beaks, and stretched out their necks;
and opening their wings, and reverently bowing their heads
to the earth, by their acts and by their songs they showed that
the words of the holy Father gave them the greatest delight.

And St. Francis rejoiced, and was glad with them, and marveled much at such a multitude of birds, and at their beautiful variety, and their attention and familiarity; for all which he devoutly praised their Creator in them. Finally, having finished his sermon, St. Francis made the sign of the Cross over them, and gave them leave to depart; and thereupon all those birds arose in the air, with wonderful singing; and after the fashion of the sign of the Cross which St. Francis had made over them, they divided themselves into four parts; and one part flew toward the east, and another to the west, another to the south, and another to the north, and all departing went their way singing wonderful songs; signifying by this, that as St. Francis, standard-bearer of the Cross of Christ, had preached to them, and made on them the sign of the Cross, after which they had divided themselves, going to the four parts of the world; so the preaching of the Cross of Christ, renewed by St. Francis, should be carried by him and by his Brothers to the whole world; and that these Brothers, after the fashion of the birds, should possess nothing of their own in this world, but commit their lives solely to the Providence of God.

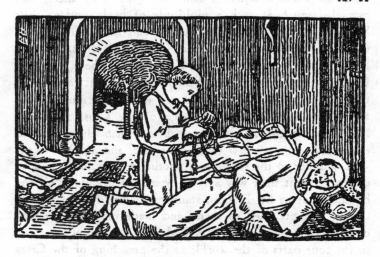

***HOW** a little boy-Brother, whilst St. Francis was
praying in the night, saw Christ and the Virgin
Mother and many other saints talking to him.*

A CERTAIN little boy, most pure and innocent, was received into the Order during the lifetime of St. Francis, and
it was in a little place where the Brothers, of necessity, slept
on truckle beds. Now once on a time, St. Francis came to
this place, and in the evening, after compline, he lay down
to sleep, that he might be able to rise in the night and pray,
when the other Brothers were asleep, according to his custom.
Then the little boy set his heart on carefully watching the
ways of St. Francis, that he might know his sanctity, and
especially that he might know what he did when he got up in

the night. And in order that he might not sleep too soundly, the boy, when he lay down by the side of St. Francis, tied his cord to the cord of St. Francis, that he might feel when he got up; and of this St. Francis perceived nothing.

But in the night, after his first sleep, when all the other Brothers slept, St. Francis arose and found his cord fastened to something, and he softly untied it, so that the boy did not feel anything, and went into the wood which was close to the house, and entering a little cell which was there, betook himself to prayer. After a while the boy awoke, and finding that the cord had been unfastened, and that St. Francis had arisen and gone away, he arose also, and went to look for him: and finding the door open, which led to the wood, he thought that St. Francis might have gone there; and entered the wood himself.

And nearing the cell where St. Francis was praying, he began to hear much speaking; and approaching nearer to see, and to make out what it was that he heard, he beheld a wonderful light, which surrounded St. Francis; and in it he saw Christ, and the Blessed Virgin Mary, and St. John the Baptist, and St. John the Evangelist, and an immense multitude of angels, who were speaking with St. Francis. Seeing and hearing all this, the boy fell to the earth as one dead. Then, the mysterious vision being ended, St. Francis, returning to the house, stumbled with his foot against the boy who lay as though dead; and in compassion, he lifted him up and carried him in his arms, as a good shepherd does with his lambs. And afterwards learning from the boy how he had seen this vision, he commanded him not to tell it to anyone, as long as he should be alive. And the boy grew in great grace with

God, and devotion to St. Francis, and became a celebrated man in the Order, and after the death of St. Francis, he revealed to the Brothers the vision which he had seen.

OF the marvelous Chapter which St. Francis held at St. Mary of the Angels, at which were present more than five thousand Brothers.

THE faithful servant of Christ, Francis, was once holding a General Chapter at St. Mary of the Angels, at which Chapter more than five thousand Brothers assembled; and there came also St. Dominic, head and founder of the Order of Friars Preachers, who was then on his way from Borgogna to Rome. And hearing of the assembling of the Chapter, which St. Francis was holding in the plain of St. Mary of the Angels, he went to see it, with seven Brothers of his Order. There was also at the said Chapter a Cardinal most devoted to St. Francis, who had prophesied to him that he should be Pope, as it afterwards came to pass. This Cardinal had come expressly from Perugia, where the Court was, to Assisi; and he came every day to see St. Francis and his Brothers, and sometimes sang the Mass, and sometimes preached to the Brothers in Chapter. The said Cardinal found the greatest delight and devotion whenever he came to visit this holy company.

And coming to the little plain of St. Mary of the Angels, he saw the Brothers grouped in companies, here forty, there a hundred, there eighty together, all occupied in speaking of the things of God, in prayer, in tears, and in exercise of charity; and this with such quietness, and such modesty, that there was not heard one sound, or any disturbance. And marveling at such a multitude, so well ordered, he said, with tears and great devotion: "Truly this is the camp and the army of the knights of God." There was not to be heard in all this multitude an idle word or unseemly jest; but wherever a company of Brothers assembled together, they either prayed, or said the Office, or wept over their own sins and those of their benefactors, or spoke of the things which are for the salvation of souls. The tents in this encampment were of willow trellis and of rush matting, and divided into groups consisting of the Brothers of the various Provinces; and hence this Chapter was called, "the Chapter of the trellises," or, "of the rush mats." Their bed was on the bare ground, with a little straw for those who had it; and for pillows, they had stones or logs of wood. For which cause, so great devotion spread from them to those who heard or saw them, and so great was the fame of their sanctity, that from the Court of the Pope, which was then at Perugia, and from the other districts of the valley of Spoleto, there came many counts, barons, and cavaliers, and other gentlemen of rank, and many parish priests, cardinals, bishops and abbots, and many other clerics, to see this so great and holy and humble congregation, like which the world had never another containing so many holy men together. And chiefly they came to see the most holy Head and Father of his holy people, who had robbed from the world so noble a prey, and assembled together so devout and fair a flock to follow in the steps of the true Shepherd Jesus Christ.

The General Chapter being therefore assembled, the holy Father and General Minister of all, St. Francis, with fervor of spirit, expounded the word of God: and preached to them with a loud voice, that which the Holy Spirit made him speak; and for the theme of his sermon, he proposed to them these words: "My sons, great are the things promised us from God: yea, too, great things are promised to us, if we observe that which we have promised to Him. Brief are the delights of this world; the pain which follows after them is perpetual: little are the pains of this life; but the glory of the other life is infinite." And on these words, he preached with the greatest devotion, comforting the Brothers, and persuading them to obey and reverence the holy Mother Church, and to have fraternal charity, to praise God for all men, and to have patience in the adversities of this world, and temperance in prosperity, and to observe modesty and angelic chastity, and to have peace and concord with God and with men, and with their own conscience, and to love and observe holy poverty. And after this, he said: "I command all you who are here assembled, by virtue of obedience, that none of you have care of solicitude for anything to eat, or anything necessary for the body: attend only to praying and praising God, and all solicitude for your body leave to Him, inasmuch as He has special care for you." And all received this command with glad hearts and with joyful countenances; and the sermon of St. Francis being ended, they prostrated themselves in prayer. At which St. Dominic, who was present during all these things, marveled greatly at the commandment of St. Francis, and considered it indiscreet, not able to think how so great a multitude should be able to govern itself, without any care or solicitude for the things necessary to the body.

But the Chief Shepherd, Christ the Blessed, willing to show how He has care for His sheep, and singular love for His poor, immediately inspired the people of Perugia, of Spoleto, of Foligno, of Spello, and Assisi, and the other surrounding districts, so that they carried what was needed to eat and drink to this holy congregation. And behold there came speedily from neighboring districts men with mules, horses and carts, laden with bread and with wine, with beans, and with cheese, and with other good things to eat, such as the poor of Christ had need of. Besides this, they brought napkins, earthen pots, bowls, drinking cups, and other vessels necessary for so great a multitude; and he considered himself blessed who could bring the most, or serve the most diligently; so that even the knights, and barons, and other gentlemen, who had come to see the sight, were the first, with great humility and devotion, to serve them.

For which cause, St. Dominic, seeing these things, and knowing of a surety that Divine Providence worked for them, humbly acknowledged that he had wrongfully judged that St. Francis had given an indiscreet commandment, and forthwith went, and kneeling down, humbly confessed his fault; and added: "Truly God has special care of these holy poor little ones, and I knew it not; and from this hour, I promise, first of all, to observe holy, evangelical poverty; and I anathematize, on the part of God, all the Brothers of my Order, who shall presume to have property." Thus was St. Dominic much edified by the faith of most holy Francis, and the obedience and poverty of so great and well-ordered a company, and by the Providence of God, and the copious abundance of all these good things.

In the same Chapter, St. Francis was told that many Brothers wore leather bands with sharp points piercing their flesh, and sharp-pointed chains of iron; from which cause many were infirm, and some were dying, and many were impeded in prayer. Whereupon St. Francis, as a wise father, commanded, by holy obedience, that those who had such leather bands, or sharp-pointed chains, should take them off, and put them down before him; and this was done; and there were counted more than five hundred iron chains with sharp points, and many more circlets, either for the arm, or the loins; so that they made a great heap; and St. Francis made them be left there. After which, the Chapter was concluded, and St. Francis, comforting them all in that which is good, and exhorting them as to how they should preserve themselves from sin in this evil world, with the blessing of God, and his own, dismissed them to their various Provinces, all consoled with spiritual delights.

HOW the vineyard of the priest of Rieti, in whose house St. Francis rested, was despoiled of its grapes, and afterwards miraculously yielded more wine than heretofore: and how God revealed to St. Francis that he should have Paradise for his portion.

IT HAPPENED once that St. Francis was suffering from a grievous malady of the eyes, and the Cardinal Ugolino, Protector of the Order, through the great tenderness which he had for him, wrote to him to come to Rieti, where were the best physicians for the eyes. Then St. Francis having received the Cardinal's letter, set out, going first to St. Damian's, where was St. Clare, that most devoted spouse of Christ, that he

might give her some consolation and thence go on to the
Cardinal. Having arrived there, the following night his eyes
grew so much worse, that he could not see the light at all;
wherefore as he could not go on, St. Clare made for him a
little cell of reeds, wherein he might rest commodiously. But
St. Francis, what with the pain of his malady, and the multitude of rats in that place, which caused him the greatest
discomfort, could get no rest either by day, or by night. And
having yet more of these pains, and sufferings to sustain, he
began to think, and to recognize that this was a chastisement
from God for his sins; and he began to return thanks to God
with all his heart, and with his mouth, and then wept aloud,
and said: "My Lord, I deserve this, and much more. My
Lord Jesus Christ, Good Shepherd, Who dost extend Thy
mercy to us sinners through divers pains and agonies of the
body, give grace and virtue to me, Thy little sheep, that by
no infirmity, or agony, or sorrow, may I be parted from Thee."

And whilst he prayed thus, there came to him a voice from
Heaven, which said: "Francis, answer Me: if all the earth
were gold, and all seas and streams and fountains were balsam,
and all mountains, hills, and rocks were made of precious
stones; and thou shouldst find another treasure more noble
than these things, even as much as gold is more noble than
earth, balsam than water, and precious stones than mountains
and rocks; and this noble treasure were given thee, through
this thine infirmity, shouldst thou not be truly glad, and well
content?" And St. Francis answered: "Lord, I am unworthy
of such precious treasures." And the voice of God said to
him: "Rejoice, Francis, because this is the treasure of Life
Eternal, which I reserve for thee until the hour when I shall
give thee the possession of it; and this infirmity and affliction

is the earnest of that blessed treasure." Then St. Francis, with the greatest joy at so glorious a promise, called his companion, and said: "Let us go to the Cardinal;" and first of all, consoling St. Clare with holy words, and taking humble leave of her, he took the road towards Rieti.

And when he was now near the city, such a multitude of people came forth to meet him, that because of them he would not enter into it, but turned aside into a church which was near to the city, about two miles off. The citizens, knowing that he was in the said church, ran together so much to see him, that the vineyard of the church was entirely spoiled, and all the grapes were plucked; at which the priest grieved much in his heart, and repented of having received St. Francis into his church. But the thought of the priest being revealed to St. Francis by God, he sent to ask him to come to him, and said: "Most beloved father, how many measures of wine did this vineyard yield thee, the year it yielded the best?" And he answered: "Twelve measures." Then said St. Francis: "I pray thee, father, to endure patiently my sojourn here for a few days, because I find here much repose; and let who will pluck the grapes of thy vineyard, for the love of God, and of me, His poor little one; and I promise thee, on the part of my Lord Jesus Christ, that it shall yield thee every year twenty measures." And such use did St. Francis make of his stay there, by the great fruit of souls, which was seen to be gathered from the people who came to him, that many went away inebriated with the Divine love, and abandoned the world.

The priest confided in the promise of St. Francis, and liberally gave up the vineyard to all who came to him. And a marvelous thing! the vineyard was altogether stripped and plucked, so that scarcely were there a few clusters of grapes to be found in it. The time of the vintage came, and the priest gathered such clusters as were left, and put them in the wine press, and trod them, and according to the promise of St. Francis obtained twenty measures of the best wine. This miraculous manifestation was intended to show that as by the merits of St. Francis, the vineyard, despoiled of grapes, abounded in wine; so the Christian people, barren of virtue through their sins, by the merits and doctrine of St. Francis, should continually abound with the good fruits of penitence.

XX

OF a wondrously beautiful vision seen by a young Brother.

A CERTAIN young man, who was of noble birth and very delicate, came into the Order of St. Francis; and from the day he entered it by the instigation of the devil, he began to have the habit which he wore in such abomination that he seemed to himself to be wearing a vile sack. He had a horror of the sleeves, he abominated the hood, and the length and roughness of the habit appeared to him an insupportable burden. And growing still more disgusted with the religious life, he at last began to entertain the thought of leaving off the habit and returning to the world.

He had acquired the custom of passing, as his master had instructed him, once in every hour before the altar of the convent where was deposited the Body of Christ, and there genuflecting with great reverence, bowing himself with his hood drawn down, and his arms crossed. And it came to pass that the night in which he was going to depart and leave the Order, he had occasion to pass in front of this altar of the convent, and in passing he genuflected according to custom and did reverence. And suddenly he was ravished in spirit, and was shown marvelous things from God; for he saw before him an innumerable multitude of saints going after the manner of a procession, two and two, clothed in the most beautiful and precious garments of fine embroidery; and their faces and their hands were resplendent as the sun, and as they went they were accompanied by hymns and songs of the angels. Among these saints were two more nobly attired and ornamented than any of the others, and they went surrounded by such a brightness that whosoever beheld them was overcome with great amazement. And at the end of the procession he saw yet another, adorned with such glory that he appeared as though he were a new-made knight more honored than all the rest. The youth, seeing this, marveled, and knew not what this procession might mean, nor had he the courage to ask, but remained rapt in ecstasy by the sweetness of the vision.

And the procession having passed by, he at last took courage and ran after those who were last in it, and with great fear asked them, saying: "O beloved ones, I pray you, may it please you to tell me what are these marvelous things that I see, and this so august procession?" And they answered him: "Know, little son, that we are all of us Friars Minor come from the glory of Paradise." And he asked them again: "Who are those two who shine more resplendently than the others?" And they answered: "Those are St. Francis and St. Anthony: and the last one, whom thou seest so much honored, is a holy Brother who died lately, whom, because he valiantly resisted temptation, and persevered to the end, we are leading to the glory of Paradise; and these garments, so beautifully embroidered as thou seest, which we wear, were given to us by God, in exchange for the rough habit which we patiently wore in religion; and the glorious brightness which thou seest in us, is given us from God for the humility and patience, and for the holy poverty, obedience, and chastity, in which we served Him unto the end. And therefore, little son, let not the wearing of the sackcloth of religion, which is so greatly rewarded, seem hard to thee; for if by the wearing of this sackcloth of St. Francis, through the love of Christ, thou despise the world, mortify the flesh, and combat valiantly against the devil, thou shalt have a vesture like to ours, and the same light of glory."

And these words said, the youth returned to himself, and much comforted by the vision he cast from him all temptation, and acknowledged his fault before the Guardian and the Brothers; and from that day forth he rather wished for the roughness of penance and coarse clothing; and finished his life in the Order, in great sanctity.

XXI

*OF the miracle which St. Francis performed when
he converted the wolf of Gubbio.*

AT THE time when St. Francis dwelt in the city of Gubbio,
there appeared in the neighborhood an enormous wolf, terrible
and ferocious, which devoured not only animals but even men
also, insomuch that all the citizens stood in great terror,
because many times he had approached the city. And all
carried arms when they went out of the city, as though they
were going to battle; yet with all this if anyone met him alone
he could not defend himself against him. And for fear of
this wolf it had come to such a pass that no one had the
courage to go out of the city. Therefore St. Francis had
compassion on the men of the place, and desired to go out to

this wolf, although all the citizens together counseled him not to do so: and making the sign of the most holy Cross he went out into the fields, he and his companions, all his confidence resting in God. And the others hesitating to go any further, St. Francis took his way to the place where the wolf was.

And behold! seeing the many citizens, who had come out to witness the miracle, the wolf made at St. Francis with open mouth. And when he had come near, St. Francis made on him the sign of the most holy Cross, and called him to him, saying: "Come along, Brother Wolf, I command thee on the part of Christ, that thou do no harm, neither to me, nor to anyone." And O wonder! immediately St. Francis had made the holy sign, the terrible wolf shut his mouth, and ceased to run, and did as he was commanded, coming gently as a lamb, and lay down to rest at the feet of St. Francis. Then St. Francis spoke to him thus: "Brother Wolf, thou hast done much damage in these parts, and many evil deeds, ravaging and killing the creatures of God, without His permission; and not only killing and devouring the cattle, but having the hardihood to destroy men made in the image of God, for which cause thou dost deserve to be hung upon the gallows like a convict, as being a thief and the worst of murderers; and all the people cry out and murmur because of thee, and the whole neighborhood is hostile to thee. But, Brother Wolf, I would make peace between them and thee, so that thou offend no more, and they shall pardon thee all past offenses, and neither men nor dogs shall persecute thee more."

At these words, the wolf, by the motions of his body and his tail and his eyes, and by inclining his head, showed that he accepted what St. Francis had said, and was ready to observe it. Then St. Francis said again: "Brother Wolf, since it pleases thee to make and to keep this peace, I promise thee that I shall have thy food given to thee continually by the men of this place, as long as thou shalt live, so that thou shalt suffer no more hunger, for I know well that it is hunger which made thee do all this evil. But since I have obtained for thee this grace, I desire, Brother Wolf, that thou promise me never more to harm man or beast; dost thou promise me this?" And the wolf by inclining his head made evident signs that he promised. And St. Francis said to him: "Brother Wolf, I would have thee pledge me thy faith that thou wilt keep this promise, without which I cannot well trust thee." And St. Francis holding out his hand to receive his faith, the wolf immediately lifted up his right paw and gently placed it in the hand of St. Francis, thus giving him such pledge of faith as he was able.

Then St. Francis said: "Brother Wolf, I command thee in the Name of Jesus Christ that thou come now with me, without doubting of anything; and let us go and confirm this peace in the name of God." And the wolf obediently went with him like a mild and gentle lamb; which the citizens saw, and marveled greatly.

And immediately the news spread over the whole city, and all the people, men and women, great and small, young and old, thronged to the piazza to see the wolf with St. Francis. And all the people being gathered together, St. Francis got up to preach, telling them among other things, how it was on account of sin that God permitted such calamities, and also pestilences. "Much more terrible," he said, "are the flames of hell, which the damned will have to endure eternally, than the fangs of the wolf, which cannot destroy more than the body. How much more then are the jaws of hell to be feared, when we see so many held in terror by the jaws of a little animal! Turn therefore, beloved, to God, and do worthy penance for your sins, and God will deliver you now from the fires of hell."

And the sermon ended, St. Francis said: "Listen, my brethren: Brother Wolf, who is here before you, has promised, and has pledged me his faith to make peace with you, and never to offend again in anything; and you will promise to give him every day that which is necessary; and I make myself surety for him, that he will faithfully observe the treaty of peace." Then all the people promised with one voice to feed him continually. And St. Francis, before them all, said to the wolf: "And thou, Brother Wolf, dost thou promise to observe and to keep the treaty of peace that thou wilt not offend either man or beast, or any creature?" And the wolf knelt down and inclined his head, and by gentle movements of his body and his tail and his ears, showed as well as he could that he was willing to keep all he had promised them. Then said St. Francis: "Brother Wolf, I desire that as thou hast pledged me thy faith to this promise outside the gates, thou wilt pledge me thy faith again before all the people, and not deceive me in the promise and guarantee which I have given for thee." Then the wolf, lifting up his right paw, placed it in the hand of St. Francis.

Whilst this and the rest that has been told above was taking place, there was such joy and admiration amongst all the people, both through devotion to the Saint, and through the novelty of the miracle, and also on account of the peace made with the wolf, that all began to cry to Heaven, praising and blessing God for sending to them St. Francis, who by his merits had delivered them from the jaws of the cruel beast. And after this, the said wolf lived two years in Gubbio; and went sociably into the houses, going from door to door without doing harm to anyone, or anyone doing harm to him, and was continually entertained by the people. And thus, as he went through fields and lanes, never did any dog bark at him. Finally, after two years, Brother Wolf died of old age: at which the citizens grieved much; for whilst he went so gently about the town, they remembered the virtue and sanctity of St. Francis.

XXII

How St. Francis tamed the wild turtledoves.

A CERTAIN youth had caught one day a great number of turtledoves; and as he was taking them to market he met St. Francis, who, having a singular compassion for these gentle creatures, looked at the doves with eyes of pity, and said to the youth: "O good youth, I pray thee give me these gentle birds, to which in the Holy Scriptures chaste and humble and faithful souls are compared; and do not let them fall into the hands of cruel men who would kill them." And immediately the young man, being inspired by God, gave them all to St. Francis; and he received them into his bosom, and said to them tenderly: "O my little sisters, simple, innocent, and chaste doves, why have you let yourselves be snared? See,

I will snatch you from death and make nests for you, wherein you may increase and multiply according to the commandment of our Creator."

And St. Francis went and made nests for them all; and they took to their nests, and began to lay eggs, and hatched them without fear before the eyes of the Brothers; and they were as tame and as familiar with St. Francis and all the other Brothers as if they had been domestic fowls always accustomed to be fed by them; and they would not depart until St. Francis with his blessing gave them leave to go. And to the young man who had given them to him, St. Francis said: "Little son, thou wilt yet be a Brother in this Order, and wilt serve Jesus Christ nobly." And so it came to pass: for the said youth became a Brother, and lived in the Order in great sanctity.

XXIII

HOW St. Francis freed a Brother who was in sin.

ONCE when St. Francis was in prayer in the House of Portiuncula, he saw the whole place surrounded and besieged by devils, as if by a great army; but not one of them could gain an entrance into the house, because the Brothers there were of such great sanctity that the devils had no means of entering. But still they persevered, till one day one of the Brothers was angered by another, and thought within his heart what accusation he could bring against him, and how he could be revenged on him; and by this means, as this evil thought remained in the Brother's mind, the devil, finding the way open to him, entered the house and placed himself on the neck of this Brother.

But the holy and watchful shepherd, who was ever watching over his flock, seeing that the wolf had entered to devour his little sheep, quickly sent one to call this Brother to him, and commanded him to disclose the venomous and odious thought which he had conceived against his neighbor, and by means of which he was now in the hands of the enemy. Upon which, affrighted at seeing that he was discovered by the holy Father, the Brother disclosed all the venomous rancor that was in him, and, acknowledging his fault, humbly begged for penance and mercy. And this done, he now being absolved from his sin, and having received his penance, immediately, before the face of St. Francis, the devil departed from him: and the Brother, thus freed from the cruel beast by the kindness of the good shepherd, gave thanks to God, and returned corrected and amended to the flock of the holy shepherd, wherein he continued to live in great sanctity.

XXIV

***HOW** St. Francis converted the Soldan of Babylon to the Faith.*

ST. FRANCIS, urged by zeal for the faith of Christ and by the desire of martyrdom, once on a time, with twelve of his holiest companions, crossed the sea, in order to go straight to the Soldan of Babylon. And they came to a country of the Saracens, where the passes were guarded by men so cruel, that never a Christian who passed that way could escape being put to death; yet as it pleased God they were not slain, but were captured, and beaten and tightly bound, and so led before the Soldan. And having come before him, St. Francis, taught by the Holy Ghost, preached so divinely of the Faith of Christ, for the sake of which he was willing even to go through the fire, that the Soldan began to have a very great devotion toward him, because of the constancy of his faith, and of the contempt of the world which he saw in him (since he would not take any gift though so utterly poor), and also because of the fervor of martyrdom, which he perceived within him. And from this time forth the Soldan listened to him willingly, and prayed him to come to him often, and gave him and his companions free leave to preach wheresoever it pleased them. And he gave them a password by using which they would be protected from being injured by anyone.

At last St. Francis, finding that he could reap no more fruit in these parts, and warned by Divine revelation, prepared to return once more to the lands of the faithful, he and all his companions; and they all came together, and went for the last time to the Soldan, to take leave of him. Then the Soldan said to him: "Brother Francis, I would willingly turn to the faith of Christ, but I fear to do so now; for if the others heard of it, they would kill both thee and myself and all thy companions; and I know that thou mayest still live to do much good; and I also have certain weighty matters to dispatch. I would not therefore at this time bring death upon thee and upon myself; but teach me how I may be saved: I am prepared to do all that which thou wilt lay upon me." Then said St. Francis: "My lord, I must now depart from thee; but after I shall have returned to my own country, and gone to heaven by God's grace, after my death, according as it shall please God, I will send thee two of my Brothers, from whom thou shalt receive the holy Baptism of Christ, and so thou shalt be saved, as has been revealed to me by our Lord Jesus Christ. And do thou meanwhile keep thyself free from all that would hinder the grace of God, that when it comes to thee it may find thee prepared for faith and devotion." And this he promised to do, and did it. Having spoken thus, St. Francis departed with the venerable company of his saintly companions; and after many years, by the death of the body, he gave up his soul to God.

And the Soldan becoming ill, and still expecting the promise of St. Francis to be fulfilled, had guards placed at certain passes, and commanded that if two Brothers should appear in the habit of St. Francis they should forthwith be brought to him. At that very time St. Francis appeared to two Brothers and commanded them to go without delay to the Soldan, and procure the salvation of his soul as he himself had promised. The Brothers departed with haste and crossed the sea, and they were conducted by the guards to the Soldan. And when he saw them he was filled with great joy, and said: "Now I know of a truth that God hath sent His servants for my salvation, according to the promise which, inspired by God, St. Francis made to me." Therefore he received instruction in the Faith, and holy Baptism, from these Brothers; and thus regenerated in Christ he died of the illness from which he was then suffering, and his soul was saved by the merits and the prayers of St. Francis.

XXV

HOW St. Francis miraculously healed the leper.

THE true disciple of Christ, St. Francis, whilst still living in this miserable life, sought with all his strength to follow Christ, the perfect Master. Wherefore it came to pass many times that the souls of those whose bodies he healed, were by Divine power also healed by God at one and the same hour, even as we read of Christ. Now he not only willingly served the lepers himself, but besides this had ordained that the Brothers of his Order, wherever they went or stayed throughout the world, should serve lepers everywhere, for the love of Christ, Who for our sakes was willing to be accounted a leper.

So it came to pass once that in a certain place near to which St. Francis then dwelt, the Brothers were serving in an infirmary for lepers and other sick, where was one leper so impatient, and so insufferably insolent that everyone believed for certain — and it was the fact — that he was possessed by the devil; because he assailed with such shameful abuse, and so showered blows upon everyone who served him, and because, what was still worse, he blasphemously reviled the Blessed Christ and His most holy Virgin Mother Mary: till at last no one could by any means be found who could or would serve him. And although the Brothers strove to bear patiently the injuries and insults leveled against themselves, that so they might increase the merit of their patience, yet those which were uttered against Christ and His Mother they could not in conscience bear, so that they determined to abandon him altogether. But they would not do this until they had mentioned the matter, according to the orders which they had received, to St. Francis who was then staying in a place close by.

And when he had heard what they had to tell, St. Francis himself went to this perverse leper, and going up to him he saluted him, saying: "God give thee peace, my beloved brother!" But the leper answered: "What peace can I have from God, Who has taken away peace and all good from me, and caused me to be covered with rottenness and to stink?" And St. Francis said: "My son, have patience, forasmuch as the infirmities of the body are given by God in this world for the salvation of the soul, because they are of great merit when borne patiently." The sick man replied: "And how can I bear patiently the continual pain which afflicts me both day and night? And I am afflicted not only by my disease, but still worse by the Brothers whom thou hast sent to serve me, and who do not serve me as they ought."

Then St. Francis, knowing by inspiration from God that this leper was possessed by the evil spirit, went and gave himself up to prayer and besought God devoutly for him. And his prayer ended he returned to the leper, and said: "Now, I will serve thee myself, since thou art not contented with the others." "As thou pleasest," said the man, "but what canst thou do for me more than the others?" And St. Francis answered him: "Whatever thou desirest, I will do." Said the leper: "I desire that thou shouldst wash me all over, because my wounds smell so foully that I cannot bear with myself." Then St. Francis quickly had water heated and many sweet-smelling herbs put into it; and after this, he stripped the leper and began to wash him with his own hands whilst another Brother poured on the water. And by Divine miracle, wherever St. Francis touched him with his holy hands the leprosy departed and the flesh became perfectly whole; and as the flesh began to heal, so the soul began to be healed also. Wherefore the leper, seeing that he was on the way to be healed, began to have great compunction and repentance for his sins and to weep bitterly; so that as the body was cleansed outwardly from the leprosy by the washing with water, so the soul was purified inwardly from sin by repentance and by tears.

And being completely healed in body and in soul, he humbly acknowledged his sin, and said weeping and with a loud voice: "Woe to me, who am worthy of hell for the injuries and insults which I have put upon the Brothers in words and deeds, and for my impatience and blasphemy against God!" And then for fifteen days he continued in bitter weeping over his sins, begging mercy of God; and meanwhile he confessed all his sins to a priest. And St. Francis, seeing so express a miracle which God had worked by his hands, returned thanks to God and departed, going thence to a far country, because from humility he would fly from all glory for himself, and because in all his works he sought the honor and glory of God only and not his own.

Then, as it pleased God, the leper healed in body and soul, after thus doing penance for fifteen days, fell sick of another malady, and fortified by the Sacraments of the Church he died a holy death: and his soul, on its way to Paradise, appeared in the air to St. Francis, who was in a wood in prayer, and said: "Dost thou know me again?" "Who art thou?" said St. Francis. "I am that leper, whom the Blessed Christ healed through thy merits; and now I am going into life eternal: for which I give thanks to God and to thee. Blessed be thou in thy soul and thy body; and blessed be thy holy words and works: because through thee many souls will be saved in the world: and know that there will never be a day while the world lasts, in which the holy angels and all the saints will not thank God for the blessed fruits which thou and thy Order will bring forth all over the world; and therefore be comforted, and give thanks to God, and may His Blessing stay with thee." And saying these words, he went to Heaven; and St. Francis remained much consoled.

XXVI

***HOW** St. Francis converted three robbers that were murderers.*

ST. FRANCIS one day was going through the desert to St. Sepulchre. And passing by a castle called Monte Casale, there came to him a youth, noble and delicate, who said to him: "Father, I would very willingly be one of your Brothers." St. Francis answered him: "My son, thou art but a youth, and delicate and noble: it may be that thou couldst not endure our poverty and hardships." And he said: "Father, are you not men as I am? therefore as you endure them, so can I, by the grace of Jesus Christ." St. Francis was much pleased with this answer; therefore blessing him, he forthwith received him into the Order, giving him the name of Brother Angelo, where he bore himself so graciously, that within a short time St. Francis made him Guardian of the House of Monte Casale.

At that time there were three noted robbers frequenting the district, who did much harm in the country round. These men came one day to the said House, and prayed the Guardian, Brother Angelo, to give them something to eat. But the Guardian reproved them harshly, answering them thus: "You, thieves and vile murderers, not ashamed to rob others of the fruits of their labors, but more than this, presumptuous and impudent that you are, you would devour the alms, which have been set apart for the servants of God; you do not even deserve that the earth should hold you, since you respect neither man, nor God Who created you; go your ways therefore, and do not show yourselves here again": at which they went away discontented and in a rage.

And behold, St. Francis came in, with a wallet of bread and a little flask of wine, which he and his companions had begged; and the Guardian telling him how he had driven the men away, St. Francis severely reproved him, saying that he had acted very cruelly: because sinners can be better brought back to God by gentleness than by harsh reproof: whence our Master, Jesus Christ, Whose Gospel we have promised to observe, has said, that the whole need not a physician, but they that are sick; and that He was not come to call the just, but sinners to repentance; and therefore also He many times ate with them. "Seeing therefore," said he, "that thou hast acted contrary to charity, and contrary to the Holy Gospel of Christ, I command thee by holy obedience, that thou immediately take this wallet of bread and this flask of wine, which I have received, and go after them with speed, and seek them over hill and valley, until thou find them, and give them all this bread and wine from me; and then kneel before them, and confess humbly thy fault in being so harsh to them; and beg them from me not to do any more evil, but to fear God and not to offend Him more: and if they will do this, I promise to provide for their wants, and to give them continually enough to eat and to drink: and when thou hast done this, return humbly to thy place."

Whilst the Guardian went to fulfill this his command, St. Francis betook himself to prayer, entreating God to soften the hearts of the robbers, and to convert them to true penitence. Having therefore overtaken them, the obedient Guardian gave them the bread and wine, and did, and said as St. Francis had bidden on him. And as it pleased God, whilst the robbers were eating the alms that St. Francis had sent them, they began to say to each other: "Woe to us, miserable wretches! how hard will be the pains of hell which we must expect, who go about, not only robbing our neighbors, and beating and wounding them, but even murdering also; and notwithstanding so many evil and shameful deeds that we have done, we have had no remorse of conscience, nor fear of God: and see how this holy Brother, who came to us but now, for a few words justly spoken against our wickedness, humbly owned himself in fault, and besides this brought us bread and wine, and so liberal a promise from the holy Father; verily these are holy Brothers and men of God, who merit Paradise; and we are sons of eternal perdition, who merit the pains of hell, and every day increase our condemnation; and we know not, after all the sins we have committed up till now, if we can return to the mercy of God."

Such and similar words one of them said to the others, who answered, "For sure thou sayest the truth, but hearken, what can we do?" "Let us go," said one, "to holy Francis; and if he gives us hope that we may find mercy with God for our sins, let us do what he commands us, and perhaps we may be able to deliver our souls from the pains of hell." This counsel pleased the others; therefore all three being agreed, they went in haste to St. Francis, and said to him: "Father, for the many shameful sins which we have done, we cannot believe that it is possible for us to return to the mercy of God; but if thou hast any hope that God would receive us to His mercy, behold we are ready to do thy bidding, and to do penance with thee." Then St. Francis, receiving them charitably and with benignity, comforted them with many examples, and assuring them of the mercy of God, promised them for certain that they should obtain it, and showed them that the mercy of God was infinite; and if that we had sins without number, yet the mercy of God is greater than our sins, according to the Holy Gospel; and the Apostle St. Paul has said: "Christ the Blessed came into the world to save sinners." Instructed by these and the like words, the said three robbers renounced the devil and his works; and St. Francis received them into the Order, and they began to do great penance, and two of them lived but a short time after their conversion, and went to Paradise.

But the third surviving, and looking back on his sins, gave himself to do such penance, that for fifteen years continually, except during Lent, which he kept in common with the other Brothers, he fasted three days in the week on bread and water, and went always barefoot, with nothing on his back but a tunic, and never slept after matins.

About this time, St. Francis departed from this miserable life. And having now for many years continued in such penance, behold there came to the aforesaid thief one night, after matins, so great a temptation to sleep, that he could not resist the inclination, nor remain watching as he ought. Finally, being neither able to resist sleep any longer nor to pray, he went to his bed in order to rest himself, but no sooner had he laid down his head, than he was ravished and led in spirit away unto a very high mountain, in which was a most profound precipice, and on this side and on that sharp and splintered rocks and broken ledges projecting from the rocks, so that the precipice was fearful to behold. And the angel who was leading this Brother pushed him on, and threw him down over the precipice, where, tumbling and rebounding, from rock to rock and from stone to stone, he at last arrived at the bottom of the precipice, and dismembered and broken to pieces, as it seemed to him. And as he lay thus on the ground, in evil plight, he that led him said to him: "Rise up, for thou must make a still greater journey." And the Brother answered: "Thou seemest to me a very indiscreet and cruel man, who, seeing me lying here almost dead from the fall which has so broken me, yet tellest me to rise." And the angel approaching him, touched him, and healed all his limbs, and restored him.

And after this, the angel showed him a great plain, full of sharp and cutting stones and thorns and brambles, and said to him that it behooved him to traverse the whole of this plain, and that he must pass over it barefooted until he came to the end, where he perceived a fiery furnace, into the which he must enter. And the Brother having passed over this plain with great pain and anguish, the angel said to him: "Enter into this furnace, for it behooves thee so to do." And he answered: "Alas! how cruel a guide thou art to me, who, seeing me near to death through the agonizing journey over this plain, biddest me now for the rest to enter this fiery furnace." And looking he saw round about the furnace many devils with iron forks in their hands, with which, while he hesitated to enter, they forced him in.

And when he had entered the furnace, looking about he saw one that had been his fellow, who was all on fire; and he asked him: "O unhappy companion, how camest thou hither?" And the other replied: "Go on a little farther, and thou wilt find my wife, thy kinswoman, who will tell thee the cause of our damnation." The Brother went farther in, and behold this said kinswoman appeared all blazing, shut up in a corn-measure all aflame; and he asked her: "O unhappy and miserable cousin, wherefore hast thou come into this cruel torment?" And she answered: "Because at the time of the great famine, which was foretold by holy Francis, my husband and I falsified the measure of the wheat and the grain which we sold; and therefore I burn here, shut up in this corn-measure."

And after these words, the angel who was leading the Brother thrust him out from the furnace, and said to him: "Prepare thyself to make a terrible journey, which thou hast yet before thee." And, he bitterly lamenting, said: "O most hard conductor who hast no compassion on me! Thou seest that I am almost burnt up in this furnace, and yet again thou wouldst lead me on a perilous and horrible journey." And the angel touched him, and made him whole and strong. And he led him to a bridge, which could not be passed without great danger, because it was exceeding frail and narrow, and very slippery, and without a railing at the sides. And beneath it flowed a terrible stream, full of serpents and dragons and scorpions, and casting forth an exceeding great stench.

And the angel said to him: "Pass over this bridge, for thou must needs do so." And he answered: "How can I pass over it without falling into this perilous stream?" And the angel said: "Follow me, and place thy foot where thou shalt see I place mine, and thou shalt pass over it well." The Brother crossed over, therefore, behind the angel, as he had instructed him, until they came to the middle of the bridge: and having come to the middle, the angel flew away, and departed from him, and went to a very high mountain afar off, on the other side of the bridge. And the Brother saw well which way the angel had gone, but remaining without a guide, and looking down below, where he saw those terrible animals, with their heads stretched out of the water, and with their jaws open, ready to devour him if perchance he should fall, he was seized with such fear and trembling that he nowise knew what to say nor what to do, because he could neither turn back nor go onwards. Wherefore seeing himself in such great tribulation, and that he had no refuge save God, he lay down, and holding on to the bridge with his arms, with all his heart and with tears he recommended himself to God, that of His most holy mercy He would succor him.

And as his prayer ended, it seemed to him that he began to put forth wings, whence he began with great joy to hope that they would grow, so that he might be able to fly from where he was on the bridge to the place where the angel had flown. But after a time, from the great desire he had to get over this bridge, he began to fly; and because his wings were not long enough, he fell down on the bridge, and the feathers drooped; wherefore he embraced the bridge as before, and recommended himself to God as at the first.

And having prayed, again he seemed to put forth wings, but as before, he did not wait till they were perfectly grown; so that attempting to fly before the time, he fell as before on the bridge, and the feathers drooped. Therefore seeing that by reason of the haste he was in to fly before the time, he fell each time, he began to say with himself: "Of a surety, if I put forth wings again the third time, I will wait long enough, until they are grown, so that I may be able to fly without falling again." And remaining in this thought, he found himself the third time putting forth wings, and waited a long time, even until they were well grown, so that it seemed to him that, with the first and second and third putting forth of his wings, he had waited a good hundred and fifty years, or more.

At the last, he raised himself the third time, and with all his strength, he took his flight, and flew up on high, even to the place where the angel had flown; and knocking at the door of the palace in which the angel was, the doorkeeper asked of him: "Who art thou that comest here?" He answered: "I am a Friar Minor." The porter said to him: "Wait, for I will bring St. Francis to see if he know thee." While he was going for St. Francis, the other began to consider the wonderful walls of this palace, and lo! they seemed translucent, and of such brightness, that he saw clearly the choirs of the saints, and all that was being done within.

And standing thus stupefied at what he beheld, behold there came St. Francis, with Brother Bernard and Brother Giles, and after them such a multitude of saints and holy women who had followed his example, that they seemed almost innumerable: and being come to the gate, St. Francis said to the porter: "Let him come in, for he is one of my

Friars." And immediately he entered, he felt such consolation and sweetness, that he forgot all the tribulations he had suffered, as though they had never been. Upon which, St. Francis leading him within, showed him many marvelous things, and afterwards said to him: "Son, thou must needs return to the world and remain there seven days, during which prepare thyself diligently with great devotion; for after the seven days are ended I will come for thee, and then thou shalt enter with me into this place of the blessed."

St. Francis was arrayed in a marvelous mantle adorned with most beautiful stars, and his five stigmas were like unto five most beautiful stars, and of such splendor that all the palace was illumined with their rays. And Brother Bernard had on his head a crown of most beautiful stars, and Brother Giles was adorned with a most marvelous light, and many other holy Friars he recognized amongst them, whom he had never seen in the world. Having taken leave therefore of St. Francis, he returned, although much against his will, to the world: and awaking and coming to himself, the Brothers were ringing for prime; so that he was in that vision only from matins until prime, although it seemed to him many years. And having recounted to his Guardian the whole of this vision in order, as it befell him, within seven days after he sickened of a fever, and on the eighth day, St. Francis according to his promise came to him, with a very great multitude of glorious saints, and led forth his soul to the Kingdom of the Blessed, and to Eternal Life.

XXVII

HOW St. Francis converted two scholars at Bologna.

As ST. FRANCIS came once on a time to the city of
Bologna, all the townsfolk ran out to see him; and so great
was the crowding of the people, that with great difficulty could
they reach the great square. And the square being full of
men and women, and of scholars, St. Francis stood up in
the midst of them, on a raised place, and preached as the
Holy Ghost inspired him; and he preached so wonderfully,
that it seemed as though it were an angel rather than a man
who was preaching. And his words appeared so heavenly, that
they were as sharp darts, which pierced the breasts of those
that heard him, so that during his preaching a great multitude
of men and women were converted to repentance.

Amongst these, there were two noble students of the March of Ancona; one was called Pellegrino, and the other Rinieri; both of whom were so touched to the heart by the Divine inspiration, through the aforesaid preaching, that they came to St. Francis, and said to him that they desired to abandon the world entirely, and to be of the number of his brethren. Then St. Francis, considering their great fervor, and knowing by revelation that they were sent by God, and that they would lead a holy life in the Order, received them with joy, saying: "Thou, Pellegrino, keep the way of humility in the Order; and do thou, Brother Rinieri, serve the brethren." And so it was; for Brother Pellegrino never would be a cleric, but became one of the lay brothers, although he was very learned and profoundly versed in the canon law; by which humility he attained to great perfection of virtue, insomuch that Brother Bernard, the first-born of St. Francis, said of him that he was one of the most perfect Friars in this world. And finally, the said Brother Pellegrino, full of virtue, closed his blessed life on earth, performing many miracles both before and after his death. And likewise Brother Rinieri devotedly and faithfully served the Brothers, living in great holiness and humility, and he became very familiar with St. Francis. And being made afterwards Minister of the Province of the March of Ancona, he ruled it during a long time, with the greatest peace and discretion.

After a while, it pleased God to permit a very great temptation to arise in his soul; for which cause, being in much trouble and anguish, he afflicted himself greatly with fasting and discipline, with tears and prayers, day and night. Nevertheless he could not banish the temptation, but oftentimes was greatly discouraged, because he reputed himself abandoned

of God. Being in this plight therefore, as a last remedy, he
determined to go to St. Francis, thinking thus within himself:
"If St. Francis shows me a good countenance, and is familiar
with me as is his wont, I will believe that God will yet have
pity on me; but if not, it will be a sign that I am abandoned
of God."

Therefore he departed, and went to St. Francis, who was
sick and sojourning, at that time, in the palace of the Bishop
of Assisi; and God revealed to him all the manner of the
temptation that had come to the said Brother Rinieri, and his
disposition, and how he was coming to him. And immediately
St. Francis called Brother Leo and Brother Masseo, and said to
them: "Go with speed to meet my most dearly beloved son,
Brother Rinieri, embrace him for me, and salute him, and
say to him that of all the Brothers that are in the world,
I love him singularly." They went therefore, and found
Brother Rinieri on the way, and embracing him, told him
that which St. Francis had commanded them; whence such
consolation and sweetness came into his soul, that he was
as one beside himself, and thanking God with all his heart,
he went on till he arrived at the place where St. Francis lay
ill. And although St. Francis was suffering from grievous
infirmity, nevertheless, when he heard Brother Rinieri coming,
he arose, and went to meet him, and most sweetly embraced
him, and said to him: "My dearest son, Brother Rinieri, of all
the Brothers that are in the world I love thee singularly."
And having thus said, he made the sign of the most holy
Cross on his forehead, and kissed him, and again he said to
him: "Dearest son, this temptation has been permitted by
God, for thy great gain of merit, but if thou dost not wish

to have this gain any longer, do not have it." O wonder! Scarcely had St. Francis pronounced these words, than immediately all the temptation left him, as if he had never in his whole life felt it, and he remained entirely consoled.

XXVIII

OF the rapture that came to Brother Bernard.

THIS great favor God oftentimes granted the poor Evan-
gelicals, who had abandoned the world for the love of Christ;
and especially showed forth in Brother Bernard of Quintavalle,
who, after he had taken the habit of St. Francis, was many
times ravished in God by the contemplation of heavenly things.
Amongst other times, it happened once, that being in church
hearing Mass, with his mind raised to God, he became so
absorbed and ravished in God, that when the Body of Christ
was being elevated, he perceived nothing, neither did he kneel,
nor take down his hood, as the others did. Looking fixedly,
but without any motion of his eyes, he remained from morning until noon unconscious, and after midday, returning to

himself, he went about the place, crying out with a voice full of admiration: "O Brothers! O Brothers! O Brothers! there is not a man in this country, were he ever so great and so noble, who, if there were promised to him a palace most beautiful and full of gold, would not willingly carry a sackful of dung in order to gain so noble a treasure."

The aforesaid Brother Bernard had his mind so elevated to this heavenly treasure promised to those who love God, that for fifteen years continually he went with his mind and his face raised to Heaven; in which time he never satisfied his hunger at table, although he always ate a little of what was placed before him; because he said that a man does not attain perfect abstinence in that which he does not relish; but the true abstinence is temperance in that which is pleasant to the palate. From this abstinence there came to him also such light and illumination of the intelligence, that even the great clerics had recourse to him for the solution of the hardest questions and the most obscure passages of scripture, and he solved every difficulty.

And because his mind was entirely free and detached from earthly things, he, like the swallows, flew high up by contemplation, so that sometimes for twenty days, sometimes for thirty days, he remained alone on the tops of the highest mountains, in the contemplation of heavenly things. Wherefore Brother Giles said of him, that to no other man was given this gift which was given to Brother Bernard of Quintavalle, namely, that he should feed flying like the swallow; and on account of this excellent favor, which he had received from God, St. Francis willingly and often spoke with him both day and night; so that sometimes they were found together, ravished in God the whole night long in the wood, where they had retired to speak together of the things of God.

XXIX

HOW *the devil appeared in the form of the Crucified on several occasions to Brother Ruffino, telling him that all the good he did was lost.*

BROTHER RUFFINO, one of the most noble citizens of the town of Assisi, a companion of St. Francis and a man of great sanctity, was at one time most powerfully assaulted and tempted in his soul, about predestination; through which he became full of melancholy and sadness, because the devil put it into his heart that he was damned, and not of those predestined to eternal life, and that he would lose that which he did in the Order. And this temptation lasting day after day, through shame he did not reveal it to St. Francis; nevertheless he did not omit to pray and use the customary abstinence, for which cause the enemy began to add to him sorrow upon sorrow, over and above the battle within, assaulting him with false apparitions. Wherefore he appeared to him at one time in the form of the Crucified, and said to him: "O Brother Ruffino, wherefore dost thou afflict thyself with penance and prayer, since thou art not of the number of those elected to eternal life? and believe me that I know whom I have elected and predestined, and do not believe the son of Peter Bernardone if he tells thee the contrary, and also do not ask him about this matter, because neither he nor anyone knows it, if not I, who am the Son of God: and therefore believe me for certain, that thou art of the number of the damned, and the son of Peter Bernardone, thy Father, and his father also, are damned, and whosoever follows him is deceived." And these words said, Brother Ruffino began to be so disheartened by the Prince of Darkness, that he lost all faith and love he had had for St. Francis, and did not care to tell him anything.

But that which Brother Ruffino did not tell the holy Father, the Holy Ghost revealed to him: wherefore St. Francis, seeing in spirit such peril to the said Brother, sent Brother Masseo for him, whom Brother Ruffino answered roughly: "What have I to do with Brother Francis?" Then Brother Masseo, all filled with the Divine wisdom, knowing the deception of the devil, said: "O Brother Ruffino, dost thou not know that Brother Francis is like an angel of God, who has illumined so many souls in the world, and through whom we have received the grace of God? therefore I will have thee come with me without delay to him, because I clearly see that thou art deceived by the devil." And this said, Brother Ruffino arose and went to St. Francis. And St. Francis seeing him coming from afar, began to cry out: "O naughty Brother

Ruffino, whom hast thou believed?" And when Brother Ruffino was come to him, he told him, in order, all the temptations that he had from the devil, both within and without, and showed him clearly that he who had appeared to him was the devil, and not Christ, and that on no account should he consent to his suggestions; "but when the devil shall say to thee again: 'Thou art damned,' answer him: 'Open thy mouth.' And this shall be the sign to thee that he is the devil, and not Christ: as soon as thou shalt have given him this answer, immediately he will fly. Again, by this token thou shouldst know that this was the devil, because he hardened thy heart against all good, which thing it is his proper office to do; but Christ the Blessed never hardens the heart of the faithful man, but rather softens it, as he has said by the mouth of the prophet: 'I will take away the heart of stone, and give them a heart of flesh.' "

Then Brother Ruffino, seeing that St. Francis told him in order all the manner of his temptation, and melted by his words, began to weep abundantly, and to give praise to St. Francis; and humbly acknowledged his fault in having hidden his temptation. And thus he remained all consoled and comforted by the admonitions of the holy Father, and all changed for the better. Then finally St. Francis said to him: "Go, son, and confess, and do not cease with diligence to pray as usual; and know that assuredly this temptation shall be of great use and consolation to thee, and in a short time thou shalt prove it."

Having returned therefore to his cell in the wood, and continuing in prayer, with many tears, behold, the enemy came to Brother Ruffino in the form of Christ as to his outward appearance, and said to him: "O Brother Ruffino, did not I say to thee that thou shouldst not believe the son of Peter Bernardone, and that thou shouldst not weary thyself with tears and prayers, seeing that thou art damned? What doth it benefit thee to afflict thyself during life, and then when thou diest, thou shalt be damned?" And suddenly Brother Ruffino answered the devil: "Open thy mouth." At which the devil, disgusted, immediately departed, with such a storm and commotion of the stones on Mount Sabassio, which was near-by, that for a great space there remained the ruins of the stones which fell down; and so great was the striking of one against another in their rolling, that they kindled terrible flashes of fire through the valley; and at the horrible noise which they made, St. Francis and his companions came out of the house, with great amazement, to see what marvel had happened; and even to this day is seen there that immense ruin of stones.

Then Brother Ruffino manifestly saw that it was the devil who had deceived him. And turning to St. Francis, he threw himself again on the ground, and acknowledged his fault; and St. Francis comforted him with gentle words, and sent him all consoled to his cell, in which, as he remained in most devout prayer, Christ the Blessed appeared to him, and in-flamed his whole soul with the Divine Love, and said: "Well hast thou done, son, that thou hast believed Brother Francis, because he that distressed thee was the devil; but I am Christ, thy Master, and to make thee well assured of it, I give thee this sign: as long as thou livest, thou shalt feel no more sad-ness or melancholy." And having thus said, Christ departed, leaving him so much joy and sweetness of spirit and elevation of mind, that day and night he was absorbed and ravished in God.

And from that time he was so confirmed in grace, and so sure of his salvation, that he was entirely changed into another man, and would have remained day and night in prayer, and in the contemplation of divine things, if the others would have let him remain. Wherefore St. Francis said of him that Brother Ruffino had been canonized in this life by Christ, and that, except in his own presence, he would not hesitate to call him St. Ruffino, although he was still living upon the earth.

XXX

OF the beautiful sermon preached in Assisi by St. Francis and Brother Ruffino.

BROTHER RUFFINO by continued contemplation was so absorbed in God, that he became almost insensible and speechless, and moreover had neither grace nor courage nor eloquence in preaching; nevertheless St. Francis commanded him one day to go to Assisi and preach to the people that which God inspired him to say. To which Brother Ruffino replied: "Reverend Father, I pray you to excuse me, and send me not, because, as thou knowest, I have not the grace of preaching, but am simple and stupid." And St. Francis said: "Since thou hast not obeyed promptly, I command thee by holy obedience, that thou go in thy breeches only

to Assisi, and enter into a church, and preach to the
people." At this command, Brother Ruffino stripped off his
habit, and went to Assisi, and entered a church, and having
made his reverence to the altar, he ascended the pulpit and
began to preach; at which the children and the men began to
laugh, and said: "Now see, these men do so much penance,
that they become fools and beside themselves."

In the meanwhile, St. Francis, thinking over the prompt
obedience of Brother Ruffino, who was one of the highest
gentlemen of Assisi, and of the hard command which he had
given him, began to reproach himself, saying: "Whence hast
thou so great presumption, son of Peter Bernardone, thou
sorry wight, to command Brother Ruffino, who is one of the
highest gentlemen of Assisi, to go and preach to the people,
as if he were a madman? By God's grace, thou shalt prove in
thyself that which thou hast commanded to others." And
immediately, in fervor of spirit, he stripped himself in like
manner, and went his way to Assisi, taking with him Brother
Leo, to carry his habit and that of Brother Ruffino. And the
townsmen of Assisi seeing him in the same plight, derided
him, declaring him and Brother Ruffino both mad, through
excess of penance.

And St. Francis entered the church, where Brother Ruffino
was preaching in these words: "O most dearly beloved, fly
the world and forsake sin; restore that which belongs to others,
if you would escape hell; keep the commandments of God,
by loving God and your neighbor, if you wish to go to
heaven; do penance, if you would possess the kingdom of
heaven." Then St. Francis ascended the pulpit, and began to
preach so wondrously of the contempt of the world, of holy
penance, of voluntary poverty, and of the desire of the

heavenly kingdom, and of the nakedness and opprobrium of the Passion of our Lord Jesus Christ, that all they that were present at the sermon, both men and women, a great multitude, began to weep bitterly, with great devotion and compunction of heart. And not only in the church, but through all Assisi that day, there was such weeping for the Passion of Christ that the like was never known.

And the people being thus edified and consoled by this act of St. Francis and Brother Ruffino, St. Francis reclothed Brother Ruffino and himself, and thus rehabited they returned to the convent of the Portiuncula, praising and glorifying God, Who had given them grace to overcome themselves by the contempt of themselves, and to edify the little sheep of Christ by good example, and to show how much the world is to be despised. And in that day, the devotion of the people increased so greatly towards them, that he reputed himself blessed who could touch the hem of their garment.

XXXI

HOW St. Francis knew the secrets of the consciences
  of all his Friars.

AS OUR Lord Jesus Christ says in the Gospel: "I know
My sheep, and they know Me:" so the blessed Father St.
Francis, as a good shepherd, knew by Divine revelation all the
merits and virtues of his companions; and so he knew their
defects; for which reason, he knew how to apply the best
remedy for such, namely, by humbling the proud, exalting the
humble, reproving vice, and praising virtue, as is to be seen in
the admirable revelations which he had concerning his primi-
tive family. Among these we find that St. Francis, being
with the said family in a certain place discoursing of God,
and Brother Ruffino not being with them in this discourse,

but being in the wood, in contemplation, whilst they continued reasoning of God — behold, Brother Ruffino came out of the wood, and passed by at a little distance from them.

Then St. Francis, seeing him, turned to his companions, and asked them, "Who, think you, is the holiest soul that God has in the world?" And they answered him, saying that they thought it was his own. Then St. Francis said: "Most beloved Brothers, I am of myself the most unworthy and the vilest man that God has in this world; but see you that Brother Ruffino, who has just now come out of the wood? God has revealed to me that his soul is one of the three most holy souls in the world; and of a surety I tell you, that I should not hesitate to call him St. Ruffino in his lifetime, for his soul is confirmed in grace, and sanctified and canonized in Heaven by our Lord Jesus Christ:" but these words St. Francis never spoke in the presence of the said Brother Ruffino.

In like manner, as St. Francis knew the faults of his brethren, he clearly saw through Brother Elias, whom he oftentimes reproved for his pride; and also Brother John della Capella, of whom he foretold that he would hang himself by the neck; and that Brother whom the devil held tightly by the throat, when he was corrected for his disobedience; and many other Brethren, whose secret defects and virtues he clearly knew by the revelations of Christ.

XXXII

***HOW Brother Masseo obtained from Christ the
virtue of his humility.***

THE first companions of St. Francis, with all their strength,
endeavored to be poor in the things of this world, and rich
in virtues by which we attain to the true heavenly and eternal
riches. It came to pass one day, that being gathered together
speaking of God, one of them spoke thus, by way of example.
There was one who was a great friend of God, and who had
great grace, both for the active and for the contemplative life,
and moreover, had such an excessive humility, that he reputed
himself the greatest sinner; the which humility sanctified and
confirmed him in grace, and made him continually to grow
in virtue and in the gifts of God, and never suffered him to

fall into sin. Brother Masseo hearing such wonderful things of humility, and knowing it to be a treasure of eternal life, began to be so inflamed with the love and the desire of this virtue of humility, that in great fervor, raising his face to Heaven, he made a vow and firm resolve never to rejoice again in this world, except in so far as he should feel this virtue to be perfectly in his soul. And from that time forth, he remained almost entirely secluded within his cell, macerating his body with fastings, vigils, and prayers, and very great abundance of tears before God, in order to obtain this virtue, without which he reputed himself worthy of hell, and with which that friend of God, of whom he had heard, was so dowered.

And remaining in this desire many days, Brother Masseo entered one day into the wood, and in fervor of spirit he went through it, shedding tears, sending forth sighs and cries, asking from God, with fervent desire, this Divine virtue. And because God willingly grants the prayers of the humble and contrite, as Brother Masseo was standing thus, there came a voice from Heaven, which called him twice: "Brother Masseo! Brother Masseo!" And he knowing in spirit, that it was the voice of Christ, answered: "My Lord!" And Christ said to him: "What wouldst thou give, to have this grace which thou hast asked?" Brother Masseo answered: "Lord, I would give the eyes out of my head." And Christ said to him: "And I will that thou have the grace and thine eyes also." And this said, the voice ceased.

And Brother Masseo remained filled with so much grace with the virtue he had desired, and with the light of God, that from this time forth he was ever in mirth and gladness; and oftentimes when he prayed, he expressed his gladness of heart in the form of a sound like that of a dove, uttering, *Coo, Coo, Coo*. And with a merry countenance, and a joyful heart, he remained thus in contemplation: and along with this, having become altogether most humble, he reputed himself the least of all men upon earth. Being asked by Brother James of Fallerone, why, in his rejoicing, he did not change his tune, he replied with great delight that when one was well contented in one thing, there was no need of change of tune.

XXXIII

***HOW St. Clare, by command of the Pope, blessed
the loaves which were on the table.***

ST. CLARE, most devoted disciple of the Cross of Christ,
and noble plant of St. Francis, was of such sanctity, that not
only Bishops and Cardinals, but the Pope himself desired,
with great affection, to see her, to hear her, and oftentimes
visited her in person. Among other times, once when the Holy
Father went to her convent, to hear her speak of heavenly
and divine things: whilst they were together, holding divers
discourses, St. Clare meanwhile had the tables prepared, and
the loaves placed on them in order that the Holy Father might
bless them. The spiritual discourse being ended, she inclined
herself with great reverence, prayed him to be pleased to bless

the loaves before their repast. The Holy Father answered: "Sister Clare, most true and faithful one, I desire that thou bless these loaves, and make on them the sign of the most holy Cross, to which thou hast entirely given thyself." St. Clare replied: "Most Holy Father, pardon me, who would be worthy of too great rebuke, if before the Vicar of Christ, I, who am a worthless woman, should presume to give this blessing." And the Pope answered: "In order that this may not be imputed to presumption, but to the merit of obedience, I command thee, by holy obedience, that thou make on these loaves the sign of the most holy Cross, and bless them in the name of God." Then St. Clare, like a true daughter of obedience, most devoutly blessed these loaves, with the sign of the most holy Cross. Wonderful to relate! immediately there appeared on all these loaves the sign of the Cross, most beautifully figured; then of these loaves, some were eaten and some miraculously preserved. And the Holy Father, having seen the miracle, took of the loaves with him, and departed, leaving St. Clare with his blessing.

At that time, there dwelt in the Convent Sister Ortolana, the mother of St. Clare, and Sister Agnes, her own sister, full of virtue and of the Holy Spirit, and many other Religious; to whom St. Francis sent many sick and infirm, and they, by their prayers, and by the sign of the most holy Cross, restored health to them all.

XXXIV

HOW St. Louis, King of France, came to visit Brother Giles.

ST. LOUIS, King of France, went on pilgrimage to visit the holy places all over the world; and hearing the exceeding great fame of the sanctity of Brother Giles, who was one of the first companions of St. Francis, he proposed in his heart, and determined at all cost, to visit him personally; for which reason he came to Perugia, where the said Brother Giles lived at that time. And coming to the door of the Community house, as a poor unknown pilgrim, with but few companions he asked with great instance for Brother Giles, not telling the porter who he was that asked. The porter therefore went to Brother Giles, and told him there was a pilgrim at the door asking for him: and God inspired him and revealed to him that it was the King of France: wherefore immediately, with great fervor of spirit, he came out of his cell and ran to the door; and without further questioning, and without even having seen each other before, with the greatest devotion, inclining themselves, they embraced, and kissed one another, with as much familiarity as though for a long while they had been together in intimate friendship: but with all this, neither one nor the other spoke. But they stood thus embracing each other, with this sign of the love of charity between them, in silence. And after they had stood thus a great space, without either speaking a word to the other, they departed from each other, and St. Louis went his way on his journey, and Brother Giles returned to his cell.

When the King was gone, one of the Brothers asked another of his companions who he was who had been so long embracing Brother Giles: and the other answered that it was Louis, King of France, who had come to see Brother Giles. Which when he had heard, the first Brother told all the others, and they were greatly grieved that Brother Giles had not spoken a word to him; and complaining, they said to him: "O Brother Giles, why hast thou shown thyself so unmannerly, when so holy a King has come from France to see thee, and to hear some good word from thy holy mouth, that thou hast not spoken to him at all?"

And Brother Giles answered: "Beloved Brothers, wonder not at this, for neither could I speak a word to him, nor he to me; because as soon as we embraced each other, the light of Wisdom revealed and manifested his heart to me, and mine to him: and thus by the Divine operation looking into each other's hearts, we knew much better what I would have said to him, and he would have said to me, than if we had spoken it with the mouth, and with more consolation, than if we had gone about to explain with the voice that which we felt in our hearts. For from the defectiveness of human language, which cannot clearly express the mysterious secrets of God, we should much more readily have discouraged than encouraged one another: and therefore know that the King took leave of me, marvelously contented and comforted in his soul."

XXXV

HOW St. Clare, being sick, was miraculously carried to the Church, and there heard the Office.

ST. CLARE was very sick once on a time, so that she could not go to say the Office in the church with the other Religious. And the day having come for the solemnity of the Nativity of Christ, all the others went to matins; and she remained in bed, sad at heart, that she could not go with the others, to have some spiritual consolation. But Jesus Christ her Spouse, not willing to leave her thus disconsolate, caused her to be miraculously carried to the Church of St. Francis, to be present during the whole of the Office of matins and of the Midnight Mass, and besides this to receive the Holy Communion, and then to be carried back to her bed.

The Religious returning to St. Clare, when the Office in St. Damian's was over, said to her: "O Mother, Sister Clare, what consolation we have had in this holy feast of the Nativity! would that it pleased God you had been with us." And Sister Clare answered: "Praise and thanks be to our blessed Lord Jesus Christ, my Sisters and most beloved daughters; because that in the solemnity of this most holy night, and more even than you, I also had part with great consolation of heart, since by the procuring of my Father St. Francis, and by the grace of our Lord Jesus Christ, I have been present in the Church of my venerable Father St. Francis, and with my bodily ease, and the ease of my mind also, I have heard all the Office, and the playing of the organ they have there; and have myself received the Holy Communion. Therefore for such a grace done me, praise and thank our Lord Jesus Christ."

XXXVI

***HOW** St. Francis explained to Brother Leo a wonderful vision that he had seen.*

Once, St. Francis was grievously sick, and Brother Leo was serving him. And as the said Brother Leo remained in prayer by the side of St. Francis, he was rapt in ecstasy, and taken away in spirit to where there was a very great stream, wide and impetuous. And as he stood, looking what would come to pass, he saw some of the Brothers enter the stream, bearing loads on their shoulders, who immediately were thrown down by the impetuosity of the stream, and drowned. Some advanced as far as a third part of the way across, some got as far as midstream, some nearly to the further bank; all of whom, through the impetuosity of the stream and the loads they carried on their backs, finally slipped down and sank.

Seeing this, Brother Leo was filled with the greatest compassion; and suddenly, whilst he thus stood, behold there came a great multitude of Brothers without any burden, and loaded with nothing which did not shine with the glory of holy poverty; and entering the stream, they passed across without any peril; and when he had seen this, Brother Leo returned to himself. Then St. Francis, feeling in spirit that Brother Leo had seen some vision, called him to him, and asked of him what he had seen. And when Brother Leo had told him all the vision in order, St. Francis said: "What thou hast seen is true: The great stream is the world; the Brothers who were drowned in the stream are those who have not followed the evangelical profession, and especially unto uttermost poverty: but they who passed over without danger are those Brothers who neither seek nor possess in this world aught that is earthly or carnal, but having only that which is necessary for food and clothing, are therewith content, following Christ naked on the Cross, and bearing the burden and the sweet yoke of Christ, and of most holy obedience, joyfully and willingly; therefore they pass with ease from this temporal life to the Life Eternal."

XXXVII

HOW Jesus Christ, at the prayer of St. Francis, con-
verted a rich and noble knight.

ST. FRANCIS, the Servant of Christ, came late one evening to the house of a great and powerful nobleman, who
received with hospitality both him and his companion, and
treated them as though they had been angels of God, with
the greatest courtesy and devotion. For which cause St. Francis
bore him great love, seeing that at their entering the house
he had embraced them as friends, and kissed them, and
then washed and wiped their feet and kissed them humbly,
and had lit a great fire, and prepared the table with many
good things, and whilst they supped continually served them
with a joyful countenance.

Now when St. Francis and his companion had eaten, this nobleman said: "Behold, my Father, I offer thee myself and my possessions: whenever you have need of tunics or mantles, or of anything whatever, buy them and I will pay for them; and see, I am ready to provide for all your wants, as by the grace of God, I can, seeing I abound in all temporal goods; and therefore, for the love of God Who has given them to me, I gladly do good to His poor." Whence St. Francis, seeing so much courtesy and good will in him, and the largeness of his offer, conceived so much love for him, that when he was departing, as he went, he said to his companion: "Verily, this nobleman, who is so mindful of and grateful toward God, and so loving and courteous towards his neighbors and the poor, would do well for our religious life and our company. Know, most dearly beloved Brother, that courtesy is one of the properties of God, Who gives His sun and rain to the just and to the unjust, by courtesy; and courtesy is the sister of charity, by which hatred is extinguished, and love is cherished. Because I have seen so much divine virtue in this man, I would gladly have him for a companion; and therefore I desire that we return one day to him, and perhaps God may have touched his heart to wish to accompany us in the service of God; and meanwhile we will pray God to put this desire into his heart, and to give him the grace to carry it into effect."

Wonderful to say, a few days after St. Francis had made his prayer, God put the desire into the heart of this nobleman; and St. Francis said to his companion: "Let us go, my Brother, to the house of our courteous host, for I have an assured hope in God that with the same courtesy he has in temporal things, he will give himself to us, and be our companion." And they went. And coming near to the house, St. Francis said to his companion: "Wait for me a little; for I will first pray to God, that He would prosper our way, and that it would please Jesus Christ to concede to us, poor and weak as we are, the noble prey which we think to snatch from·the world, by the virtue of His most holy Passion." And having thus said, he disposed himself to prayer, in a place where he might be seen by the said courteous man.

Now, as it pleased God, looking hither and thither he saw St. Francis standing in prayer most devoutly before Christ, Who, in great brightness, appeared to him in this his prayer, and stood before him; and standing thus, he saw St. Francis lifted bodily above the earth for a good space. By which thing he was so touched and inspired of God to forsake the world, that immediately he came forth from his palace. And in fervor of spirit he ran towards St. Francis; and coming up to him, as he remained in prayer, knelt at his feet, and with great instance and devotion he prayed that it would please him to receive him to do penance with those of his company. Then St. Francis, seeing that his prayer was heard of God, and that this nobleman asked with great instance what he himself desired, lifted him up, and in fervor and joy of spirit embraced and kissed him, most devoutly returning thanks to God, Who had added such an accomplished knight to his company. And the nobleman said to him: "What dost thou command me to do, my Father? Behold I am ready to do thy bidding, and to give to the poor whatever I possess, and to follow Christ with thee, thus disburdened of all temporal things."

And thus he did, by the counsel of St. Francis, distributing all that he possessed to the poor; and entered the Order, and lived in great penitence and holiness of life, and virtuous conversation.

XXXVIII

HOW St. Francis knew in spirit that Brother Elias was damned, and was to die out of the Order: for which cause he prayed for him, and his prayer was answered.

As ST. FRANCIS and Brother Elias were dwelling once in a place together, it was revealed by God to St. Francis that Brother Elias was damned, and was to apostatize, and finally to die out of the Order. For which cause St. Francis conceived so great an aversion from him that he would never converse with him, nor speak to him; and if it happened at any time that Brother Elias went towards him, he turned another way, and went elsewhere to avoid meeting him; so that Brother Elias began to perceive and to understand that

St. Francis was displeased with him. Therefore, wishing to know the cause, he accosted St. Francis one day, wishing to speak with him, and St. Francis still turning away from him, he gently held him back by force, and began courteously to entreat him that it would please him to reveal the cause why he shunned his company, and avoided speaking with him.

And St. Francis answered him: "The cause is this: because it has been revealed to me by God that for thy sins thou wilt apostatize from the Order, and wilt die out of the Order; and over and above this, God has revealed to me, that thou wilt be damned." Hearing this, Brother Elias thus replied: "My reverend Father, I beg thee for the love of Jesus Christ, that thou shun me not for this, nor spurn me from thee, but as a good shepherd, after the example of Christ, bring back and receive the sheep that would perish without thine aid; and pray God for me that, if it be possible, He may revoke the sentence of my damnation; because it is written that God will change His sentence, if the sinner amend him of his sins; and I have so great faith in thy prayers, that if I were in the midst of hell, and thou didst pray God for me, I should feel some refreshment. Therefore again I beseech thee, recommend me, sinner as I am, to God, Who came to save sinners, that He would receive me to His mercy." And this Brother Elias said with great devotion, and with tears; therefore St. Francis, as a compassionate father, promised to pray to God for him; and he did so.

And as he prayed most devoutly for him, he understood by revelation that God had heard his prayer, so far as to revoke the sentence of damnation against Brother Elias, so that at the last his soul should not be damned; but that still of a surety he would leave the Order, and out of the Order he would die; and so it came to pass. For Frederick, the King of Sicily, having rebelled against the Church, and being excommunicated by the Pope — he, and all who had counseled him and aided him — the said Brother Elias, who was reputed one of the most learned men in the world, being asked by this King Frederick, went over to him, and rebelled against the Church, and apostatized from the Order; for which cause he was excommunicated by the Pope, and deprived of the habit of St. Francis.

And being thus excommunicated, and grievously sick, one of his brethren, a lay Brother, who had remained in the Order, and was a man of good and virtuous life, hearing of his sickness, went to visit him, and after some other words, said to him: "My most beloved Brother, it grieves me sore that thou shouldst be excommunicated, and cast out of thine Order, and that thou shouldst die thus; but if thou seest way or means by which I could deliver thee from this peril, willingly would I take for thee any pains." And Brother Elias answered: "My Brother, I see no other way unless thou go to the Pope, and beg him for the love of God, and of St. Francis, His servant, through whose teaching I abandoned the world, that he would absolve me from his excommunication, and restore to me the habit of Religion." And his Brother said that he would willingly take such pains upon himself, for his salvation.

And departing from him, he went on foot to the Holy Father, humbly praying him that he would do grace to his Brother, for the love of Christ and St. Francis, His servant. And as it pleased God, the Pope consented that he should return, and if he found Brother Elias alive, should absolve him, in his name, from the sentence of excommunication, and restore to him the habit. Therefore he departed joyfully, and with great haste returned to Brother Elias, and found him alive, but almost at the point of death, and absolved him from his excommunication. And Brother Elias, having put on the habit again, departed this life, and his soul was saved by the merits of St. Francis, and by his prayer, in which Brother Elias had placed such great hope.

XXXIX

OF the wonderful discourse which St. Anthony of Padua made in the Consistory.

THAT wonderful vessel of the Holy Spirit, St. Anthony of Padua, one of the chosen disciples and companions of St. Francis, whom the latter called his Vicar, was preaching once before the Pope and the Cardinals in the Consistory. And there were present men of divers nations, — Greeks, Italians, French, Germans, Slavonians, English, and others; and he was so inflamed by the Holy Spirit, and explained the word of God so devoutly, so sweetly, so clearly, and in a manner so efficacious and so learned, that all those who were in the Consistory, though they spoke different languages, understood what he said as perfectly as if he had spoken the language of each. And they were all full of wonder, for it seemed to them as if the miracle of the Apostles at the time of Pentecost had been renewed, when the Holy Spirit taught them to speak all languages; and they said among themselves, "Does not he that preaches come from Spain? How is it, then, that we each hear in his words our own tongue spoken?" And the Pope, as much surprised as the others, considering the deep meaning of his words, exclaimed, "In truth this man is the ark of the Testament, and the treasure of Holy Scripture."

XL

OF the miracle which God performed when St. Anthony preached to the fishes.

CHRIST the Blessed was pleased to show forth the great sanctity of His most faithful servant St. Anthony, and how men ought devoutly to listen to his preaching, by means of creatures without reason. On one occasion among others, He made use of fishes to reprove the folly of faithless heretics, just as we read in the Old Testament how in ancient times He reproved the ignorance·of Balaam by the mouth of an ass.

St. Anthony being at one time at Rimini, where there were a great number of heretics, and wishing to lead them by the light of faith into the way of truth, preached to them for several days, and reasoned with them on the faith of Christ and on the Holy Scriptures. They not only resisted his words, but were hardened and obstinate, and refused to listen to him. At last St. Anthony, inspired by God, went down to the sea-shore, where the river runs into the sea, and having placed himself on a bank between the river and the sea, he began to speak to the fishes as if the Lord had sent him to preach to them, and said, "Listen to the word of God, O you fishes of the sea and of the river, as the faithless heretics refuse to do so!"

No sooner had he spoken these words than suddenly a great multitude of fishes, both small and great, approached the bank on which he stood, and never before had so many been seen in the sea or in the river; all kept their heads out of the water, and seemed to be attentively looking on St. Anthony's face; all were ranged in perfect order and most peacefully, the smaller ones in front near the bank, after them came those a little bigger, and last of all, where the water was deeper, the large ones.

When they had placed themselves in this order, St. Anthony began to preach to them most solemnly, saying, "My brothers the fishes, you are bound, as much as it is in your power, to return thanks to your Creator, Who has given you such a noble element for your dwelling; for you have at your choice sweet water and salt water; you have many places of refuge from the tempest; you have likewise a pure and trans-parent element for your nourishment. God, your bountiful and kind Creator, when He made you, ordered you to increase and multiply, and gave you His blessing. In the universal deluge, all other creatures perished; you alone did God pre-serve from all harm. He has given you fins to enable you to go where you will. To you was it granted, according to the

commandment of God, to keep the prophet Jonas, and after
three days to throw him safe and sound on dry land. You it
was who gave the tribute money to our Savior Jesus Christ,
when, through His poverty, He had nothing to pay. By a
singular mystery, you were the nourishment of the Eternal
King, Jesus Christ, before and after His resurrection. Because
of all these things you are bound to praise and bless the Lord,
Who has given you so many and so much greater blessings
than to other creatures."

At these words the fishes began to open their mouths
and bow their heads, and endeavored as much as was in their
power to express their reverence and show forth their praise.
St. Anthony, seeing the reverence of the fishes towards their
Creator, rejoiced greatly in spirit, and said with a loud voice,
"Blessed be Eternal God; for the fishes of the sea honor
Him more than men without faith, and animals without reason
listen to His word with greater attention than sinful heretics."
And whilst St. Anthony was preaching, the number of the
fishes increased, and none of them left the place he had chosen.

And the people of the city, hearing of the miracle, made
haste to go and witness it. With them came the heretics of
whom we have spoken above, who, seeing such a wonderful
and manifest miracle, were touched in their hearts; and all
threw themselves at the feet of St. Anthony to hear his
words. The Saint then began to expound to them the Catholic
Faith. He preached so eloquently that all those heretics were
converted, and returned to the true faith of Christ; the faithful were filled with joy, and greatly comforted, and strength-
ened in the faith. After this St. Anthony sent away the
fishes, with the blessing of God; and they all departed, re-

joicing as they went, and the people returned to the city. St. Anthony remained at Rimini for several days, preaching and reaping much spiritual fruit in the souls of his hearers.

XLI

HOW *the venerable Brother Simon delivered a Brother from a great temptation.*

ABOUT the beginning of the Order, and during the life-time of St. Francis, a young man from Assisi, whose name was Simon, took the habit; and the Lord adorned him with such graces and such elevation of mind, that all his life he was a mirror of sanctity, as I heard from those who had lived with him for a long time. He very seldom left his cell, and whenever he was in company with the Brothers he always spoke of God. He had never learned grammar, and yet he talked of divine things and of the love of Christ in a way so elevated and with such profound wisdom, that his words seemed to be supernatural.

One evening he went into the wood with Brother James of
La Massa to speak of God; and they spent the whole night
conversing sweetly on Divine love. When morning dawned
they seemed to have been together but a few minutes, as was
related to me by the aforesaid Brother James. And Brother
Simon received the illuminations of the Divine charity with
such inward delight and sweetness of spirit, that oftentimes,
when he felt them coming, he laid himself down in his bed;
because the tranquil sweetness of the Holy Spirit produced in
him not only repose of spirit but of the body also; and in
these Divine visitations he was many a time rapt in God, and
became altogether insensible to the things of the body.

Now once when he was thus rapt in God, insensible to
the world, and inwardly burning with Divine love, without
consciousness of external things through his bodily senses, a
Brother, wishing to prove if this were so, and to see if he
truly was as he seemed to be, went and took a live coal from
the fire, and placed it upon his naked foot. And Brother
Simon felt nothing and it made no mark on his foot, although
it remained there so long that it went out of itself. The said
Brother Simon, when he placed himself at table, before taking
food for the body, both took and gave spiritual food, speaking of God.

Once by his fervent conversation, he converted a young
man of San Severino, who was an exceedingly vain and worldly
youth of that time, of noble blood, and very delicate of body.
And Brother Simon, having received the young man into the
Order, put by his secular clothes, and kept them in his own
charge; and he remained with Brother Simon, to be instructed
in the regular observance. But the devil, who busies himself
to thwart all good, loaded him with ardent temptations and

stings of the flesh, which he could by no means resist; therefore he came to Brother Simon, and said: "Give me back my clothes which I wore in the world, for I can no longer resist this temptation." And Brother Simon, having great compassion for him, said: "Sit down a little, my son, with me;" and began to speak of God in such a manner, that the temptation went away; and when the temptation returned, and he asked again for his clothes, Brother Simon still banished it by talking of God.

And when this had happened several times, finally one night the said temptation assailed him so violently that for nothing in the world could he resist it; and he went to Brother Simon to demand back his secular clothes, because that noways could he remain any longer. And Brother Simon, as he was wont to do, made him sit down beside him, and spoke to him of God, till the youth leant his head on the bosom of Brother Simon, weeping for grief and sadness of heart. Then Brother Simon, for the great compassion he had for him, lifted his eyes to Heaven, and made supplication; and praying to God with the greatest fervor for him, he was presently rapt in ecstasy, and his prayer was heard of God. And when he returned to himself, the young man felt himself entirely freed from this temptation, as though he had never experienced it.

Thus was the fire of temptation exchanged for the fire of the Holy Spirit, because it had approached to the burning coal, namely to Brother Simon, who was inflamed with the love of God and his neighbor. So much so, that once, when a malefactor had been taken who was to have both his eyes put out, the aforesaid youth, filled with compassion, went with haste to the Governor, and in open council, and with many tears and devout prayers, begged that they would put out one of his eyes, and one only of the malefactor's, so that he might not remain deprived of his sight. But the Governor and the Council, seeing the great charity of this Brother, forgave both the one and the other.

Once, when Brother Simon was in the wood in prayer, and feeling great consolation in his soul, a flock of crows began to annoy him with their cries: wherefore he commanded them, in the name of Jesus, to depart and return no more: and those birds forthwith departing, from that time forward were never seen or heard either there or in all the country round. And this miracle was known in all the Province of Fermo, in which that Community dwelt.

XLII

OF the glorious miracle which God worked by the hands of some holy Brothers; and how St. Michael appeared and spoke to one of them, and the Blessed Virgin Mary came to the other.

THE Province of the March of Ancona was formerly adorned, as the firmament with its stars, with Saints and exemplary Brothers, who, like the stars of heaven, have illuminated and adorned the Order of St. Francis, and the world, with their example and their doctrine. Among the rest, there was first of all Brother Lucide Antico, who was truly resplendent with sanctity, and burning with Divine charity; whose glorious tongue, inspired by the Holy Spirit, brought forth marvelous fruit in preaching. Another was Brother

Bentivoglio of San Severino, who was seen by Brother Masseo, lifted up in the air for a great space, whilst he was in prayer in the wood; through which miracle the devout Brother Masseo, being at the time parish priest, left his parish and became a Friar Minor, and of so great sanctity that he worked many miracles, both living and dead; and his body reposes at Murro.

The above-mentioned Brother Bentivoglio, whilst sojourning once alone at Trave Bonanti, in order to take charge of and serve a certain leper, received commandment from his superior to depart thence, and go unto another place which was about fifteen miles distant. And not willing to abandon the leper, he took him with great fervor of charity, and placed him on his shoulders, and carried him, from the dawn till the rising of the sun, all the fifteen miles of the way, even to the place where he was sent, which was called Monte Sancino; which journey, if he had been an eagle, he could not have flown in so short a time; and this divine miracle put the whole country round in amazement and admiration.

Another was Brother Peter of Monticello, who was seen by Brother Servodio of Urbino, then Guardian of the old Community House of Ancona, raised bodily five or six cubits above the ground, as high as the feet of the crucifix of the church, before which he was in prayer. And this same Brother Peter, having fasted with great devotion during the forty days' fast of St. Michael, on the last day of the fast, whilst at his prayers in the church, was overheard by a young Brother (who was constantly hiding under the high altar, in order to observe some token of his sanctity) talking with St. Michael the Archangel, and the words they were saying were these. St. Michael said: "Brother Peter, thou hast faithfully given

thyself much pain for me, and in many ways afflicted thy body; lo! I am come to comfort thee, and therefore ask what grace thou wilt, and I will obtain it for thee from God." Then Peter answered: "Most holy Prince of the heavenly host, and most faithful promoter of the Divine love, and pious protector of souls, I beg of thee this grace — even to obtain for me from God the pardon of my sins." And St. Michael replied: "Ask some other favor, for this grace I will obtain for thee most easily." And Brother Peter not asking him anything further, the Archangel concluded: "By the faith and devotion thou hast toward me, I will obtain for thee this grace that thou hast asked, and many others." And having ended their speaking, which lasted for a great while, the Archangel St. Michael departed from him, and left him consoled exceedingly.

In the lifetime of this Brother Peter there lived also the holy Brother Conrad Offida, who was in the same Community House at Forano, in the Province of Ancona. The said Brother Conrad went one day into the wood for contemplation of God, and Brother Peter secretly followed him to see what would happen. And Brother Conrad began to be absorbed in prayer, and most fervently with great devotion, besought the Holy Virgin Mother that she would obtain for him this grace from her Blessed Son, that he might feel a little of that sweetness which St. Simeon felt on that day of the Purification, when he held in his arms the Blessed Savior Jesus. And having thus made his prayer, the merciful Virgin Mary granted it; and behold there appeared the Queen of Heaven, with her Blessed Son in her arms, surrounded by an exceeding great and clear light. And approaching Brother Conrad, she placed that Divine Son in his arms, who received Him with tenderest devotion, embracing and kissing Him and pressing Him to his breast, totally dissolved and melted away in the Divine love, and in unspeakable consolation. And Brother Peter likewise, who saw all these things from his concealment, felt his soul filled with the greatest sweetness and consolation.

And when the Blessed Virgin Mary had departed from Brother Conrad, Brother Peter returned with haste to the house, in order not to be seen by him. But nevertheless, when Brother Conrad came in, all full of joy and mirth, Brother Peter said to him: "O what heavenly and great consolation hast thou had today!" Then said Brother Conrad, "What is it thou sayest, Brother Peter? and what dost thou know about what I have had?" "Well do I know, well do I know," quoth Brother Peter, "how the Virgin Mother with her Blessed Son has visited thee." Then Brother Conrad, who, being truly humble desired to keep the grace of God secret, prayed him that he would tell it to no one; and such was the great love thenceforth between these two, that they seemed to have one heart and one soul between them in everything. And the same Brother Conrad once, whilst in the Community House of Siruolo, by his prayers freed a woman who was possessed, praying for her the whole of one night; and after, being seen by her mother, in the morning he escaped, in order that he might not be found and honored by the people.

XLIII

*HOW Brother Conrad of Offida converted a young
  Brother, being importuned by the other Brothers because of him; and how the said youthful
  Brother, dying, appeared to Brother Conrad,
  entreating that he would pray for him.*

THE said Brother Conrad of Offida, full of holy zeal for
Evangelical Poverty, and the Rule of St. Francis, was of so
religious a life, and of so great merit before God, that the
Blessed Lord Christ honored him both in his life and in his
death with many miracles; among which it came to pass once,
that being come to the Community House at Offida as a guest,
the Brothers prayed him, for the love of God and of charity,
to admonish a young Brother that was in the house, who

behaved so childishly and disorderly that he disturbed both old and young of the Community in saying the Divine Office and in the other regular observances, and cared little or nothing that he did so.

Therefore Brother Conrad, moved with compassion for the man and by the prayers of the Brothers, took him apart one day, and in the fervor of charity spoke to him such efficacious and holy words of instruction, that by the operation of Divine grace the youth was suddenly turned from a child into an elder in manners, and became so obedient and gentle and careful and devoted, and afterwards so peaceable and serviceable and so studious of all virtue, that, as at first all the family were disturbed by him, so now all were contented and consoled by him, and they loved him greatly.

It came to pass, as it pleased God, that soon after his conversion the young man died, at which the other Brothers sorrowed very much. And a little while after his death, his soul appeared to Brother Conrad, as he was praying fervently before the altar in the said Convent, and saluted him reverently as "Father"; and Brother Conrad asked: "Who art thou?" And the other said: "I am the soul of that young Brother who died this day." And Brother Conrad said: "O my son most beloved, how is it with thee?" And he answered: "By the grace of God, and by your instructions, so far well, inasmuch as I have escaped damnation, but indeed for my sins, which I had not time to purge sufficiently, I suffer the exceeding great pains of purgatory; but I pray thee, Father, that as by thy pity thou didst succor me whilst I yet lived, so now it may please thee to help me in my pains, saying for me some *Pater nosters*, because thy prayer is very acceptable in the sight of God."

Then Brother Conrad, consenting with benignity to his request, and having said for him once the *Pater noster*, with the *Requiem æternam*, the soul cried: "O most beloved Father, how well and how refreshed I feel myself! now, I pray thee, say it once again." And Brother Conrad said it; and when he had done so, the soul said to him: "Holy Father, when thou prayest for me, I feel my pains lightened; therefore I pray thee that thou cease not to pray for me." Then Brother Conrad, seeing that this soul was so much helped by his prayers, said for him a hundred *Pater nosters;* and when he had done so, the soul said to him: "I return thee thanks, most dear Father, in the name of God and of holy charity, because by thy prayers thou hast delivered me from all pains, and I am going to the heavenly kingdom." And so saying the soul departed. Then Brother Conrad, to give comfort and joy to the other Brothers, related to them in order the whole vision. And thus the soul of this youth went to paradise through the merits of Brother Conrad.

XLIV

***HOW the Mother of Christ appeared to Brother
Conrad, with St. John Evangelist, and told him
which of them bore most pain in the Passion
of Christ.***

AT THE time when there dwelt together in the Province
of Ancona, at the Community House of Farona, Brother
Conrad, and the before-mentioned Brother Peter, who were
two heavenly men, and two shining stars in all that province,
there was so great charity between them, that they seemed to
be one heart and one soul. And they bound themselves together to this compact: that every consolation which the mercy
of God gave to either of them, they would own it to each
other in charity and reveal it the one to the other.

This compact being made between them, it came to pass one day that Brother Peter, being in prayer, and thinking with the deepest devotion over the Passion of Christ, and how the most Blessed Mother of Christ, and St. John Evangelist, the most beloved Disciple, and St. Francis, were depicted at the foot of the Cross, by mental grief crucified with Christ, there came to him the desire to know which of the three had the greatest grief in the Passion of Christ: whether the Mother who bore Him, or the Disciple who had slept upon His breast, or St. Francis who was crucified with the wounds of Christ. And as he continued in this devout reflection, there appeared to him the Virgin Mother, with St. John Evangelist, and with St. Francis, arrayed in the noblest vestures of beatific glory; but St. Francis appeared arrayed in yet more beautiful vesture than St. John.

And as Peter stood amazed at this vision, St. John consoled him, and said to him: "Be not afraid, most beloved Brother, for we have come to console thee in thy doubt. Know then, that the Mother of Christ and I, above all other creatures, grieved over the Passion of Christ; but after us, St. Francis had greater grief than all others; and therefore thou seest him in so much glory." And Brother Peter asked him: "Most holy Apostle of Christ, why does the raiment of St. Francis appear more beautiful than thine?" and St. John answered: "The reason is this: because whilst he was upon earth he wore a viler raiment on his back than I did." And having said these words, St. John gave Brother Peter a glorious vesture, which he carried in his hand, and said to him: "Take this vesture, which I have brought to give to thee." And as St. John would have arrayed him in it, Brother Peter, stupefied, fell to the earth, and began to cry: "Brother

Conrad! Brother Conrad, most beloved! run hither to me
quickly; come, and see a marvelous thing;" and as he said
these words, the holy vision disappeared. Then Brother
Conrad coming to him, he told him these things in order: and
they returned thanks to God.

XLV

*OF the conversion, and life, and miracles, and death
of the holy Brother John della Penna.*

To BROTHER John della Penna while yet a child, and a
secular in the Province of the Marches, there appeared one
night a Child most fair and beautiful, who called him, saying:
"John, go to St. Stephen's, where one of the Friars Minor
is preaching; believe his doctrine and give heed to his words,
because I have sent him; and this done thou must make a long
journey, and then thou shalt come to me." Which hearing,
he immediately arose, and felt a great change within his soul.

And he went his way to St. Stephen's, and found a great
multitude of men and women, who were gathered together to
hear the preaching. And he who was to preach was a Brother
named Philip, who was one of the first Brothers who had
come into the Marches of Ancona, and they had as yet but
few houses in Ancona. Brother Philip therefore stood up to
preach, and preached with the greatest fervor, not with words
of human wisdom, but by the virtue of the Spirit of Christ,
announcing the Kingdom of Life Eternal.

And the sermon being ended, the aforesaid child went to
him, and said: "Father, if it please thee to receive me into
the Order, I would willingly do penance, and serve our Lord
Jesus Christ." Then Brother Philip, seeing a marvelous innocence and a ready will to serve God in the child, said to him:
"Come to me on such a day, at Ricanati, and I will have thee
received;" in which place, the Provincial Chapter was to be
held. Whereupon the child, being most pure of heart, thought
that this was the great journey he was to make, according to

the revelation he had had, and that then he should go to
paradise; and this therefore he thought to do, as soon as he
was received into the Order. He went therefore, and was
received; and seeing that his thoughts were not fulfilled then,
and the Minister in Chapter having said, that whoever would
wish to go into the Province of Provence by the merit of holy
obedience, he would willingly give him permission, there then
came to him a great desire to go, thinking in his heart that
this was the great journey which he must make before he
could go to paradise. But being ashamed to speak of it, at last
he confided all to Brother Philip, who had caused him to be
received into the Order, and begged him earnestly to obtain
for him this favor, that he should go into the Province of
Provence. Then Brother Philip, seeing his purity and his
holy intention, obtained for him this permission. Whereupon
Brother John, with great joy, set off and went, having this
belief, that when he had accomplished that journey he should
go to paradise.

But as it pleased God, he remained in that province twenty-
five years, in the same expectation and desire, showing the
greatest honesty of life and example, growing always in favor
with God and with the people, and exceedingly beloved of
the Brothers and the seculars. And as he was praying devoutly
one day, and weeping and lamenting because his desire was
not fulfilled, and his pilgrimage of this life was too much
prolonged, Christ the Blessed appeared to him, at the sight
of Whom his soul entirely melted away. And He said to
him: "Son, Brother John, ask of Me what thou wilt." And
he answered: "My Lord, I know not what to ask Thee but
Thyself, for I desire nothing besides: but this only I pray
Thee, that Thou pardon me all my sins, and give me this

grace, to see Thee another time, when I shall have the greater need." And Jesus said: "Thy prayer is granted." And this said, He departed, and Brother John remained full of consolation.

At last, the Brothers of the Marches, hearing the fame of his sanctity, exerted themselves so much with the General that he sent him his obedience that he should return to the Marches; and having received this obedience he joyfully went on his way, thinking that at the end of the journey he should go to heaven, according to the promise of Christ. But when he had returned to the Province of the Marches, he lived there thirty years; and he was not recognized by any of his relatives, and every day he waited for the mercy of God, that He would fulfill His promise to him. And in this time he fulfilled the office of Guardian several times, with great discretion; and God performed many miracles through him. And amongst other gifts which he had from God, he had the spirit of prophecy.

Now once on a time, being abroad from the house, one of his novices was assaulted by the devil, and so strongly tempted that, consenting to the temptation, he deliberated within himself to leave the Order, so soon as Brother John should have returned from without. All of which temptation and deliberation being made known to Brother John, by the spirit of prophecy, he returned home immediately, and called to him the said novice, and bade him confess himself. But before he confessed, he related to him in order all his temptation as God had revealed it to him and concluded thus: "Son, because thou hast waited for me, and wouldst not depart without my blessing, God has given thee this grace, that never shalt thou go out of this Order, but thou shalt die in the

Order, and in the grace of God." Then this novice was confirmed in good will, and, remaining in the Order, became a holy Brother: and all this was related to me by Brother Ugolino.

The same Brother John, who was a man of glad and peaceful soul, rarely would speak, but was a man given to great devotion and prayer, and especially after matins, he would never return to his cell, but remain in the Church until daylight in prayer. And as he prayed thus one night after matins, an angel of God appeared to him, and said to him: "Brother John, thy lifetime is accomplished, in which thou hast waited so long; and therefore I announce to thee from God, that thou mayest ask what grace thou wilt. And I announce to thee besides, that thou mayest choose which thou wilt — one day in purgatory, or seven days' pain on earth." And Brother John choosing rather seven days of pain in this world, immediately sickened of various infirmities, so that he was oppressed with great fever, and with gout in his hands and feet, and with pains in his side, and many other illnesses. But that which was worst of all to him was, that a devil stood in front of him, holding in his hand a great scroll, inscribed with all the sins he had ever done, or thought; and said to him: "For these thy sins, which thou hast committed by thought, word or deed, thou art damned to the lowest depths of hell." And he could not remember any good that he had done, either in the Order, or ever elsewhere, but thought for this to be damned, as the devil said to him. Therefore, when any asked him how he fared, he answered: "Ill, for I am damned."

The Brothers seeing this sent for an old Brother, called Brother Matthew of Monte Rubbiano, who was a holy man, and a great friend of Brother John's; and the said Brother Matthew came to him, on the seventh day of his tribulation, and saluted him, and asked how it was with him; and he answered, it was ill with him, because he was damned. Then Brother Matthew said: "Dost thou not remember that thou hast many times confessed thyself to me, and that I entirely absolved thee from all thy sins? Dost thou not remember also, that thou hast ever served God in this holy Order for many years? Lastly, dost thou not remember that the mercy of God exceeds all the sins of the world, and that the Blessed Christ our Savior paid an infinite price to redeem us? And therefore have good hope, that of a certainty thou shalt be saved." And as he said this, because the term of his purgation was accomplished, the temptation went, and consolation came. And with great joy Brother John said to Brother Matthew: "Because thou hast fatigued thyself and the hour is late, I pray thee go and rest thyself." And Brother Matthew was not willing to leave him, but finally, as he pressed him much, he left him, and went to lie down; and Brother John remained alone with the Brother who served him. And lo! Christ the Blessed came, in glory and splendor, and with an exceeding sweetness of fragrance, according as He had promised him to appear to him another time when he should have the greater need, and healed him perfectly of all his infirmities.

Then Brother John, with clasped hands, thanked God that he had made so good an end of the great journey of this present miserable life, in the arms of Christ, to Whom he commended his soul, passing from this mortal life to the Life Eternal with Christ the Blessed, Whom he had for so long a time desired and waited to see. And the said Brother John rests in the Convent della Penna.

XLVI

***HOW** Brother Pacificus, being in prayer, saw the soul of Brother Humilitas, his brother, going up to heaven.*

IN THE aforesaid Province of the Marches, after the death of St. Francis, there were two brothers in the Order together; the one named Brother Humilitas and the other Brother Pacificus, and they were men of very great sanctity and perfection. One, namely Brother Humilitas, was placed in the Community House at Soffiano, and there also he died: and the other belonged to another Community at some distance thence. As it pleased God, Brother Pacificus, being alone one day in prayer in a solitary place, was rapt in ecstasy, and saw the soul of his brother, Brother Humilitas, at the moment of its departure from the body, go straight to heaven, without any let or hindrance whatever.

And it came to pass that after many years Brother Pacificus, who still survived, was placed in the Community of the same House at Soffiano where his brother had died. At this time, the Brothers, at the request of the lords of Bruforte, moved from their House into another; wherefore they took away with them, among other things, the relics of the holy Brothers who had died in this House. And coming to the sepulchre of Brother Humilitas, his brother, Brother Pacificus, gathered his bones, and washed them in good wine, and then wrapped them in a white cloth; and with great reverence and devotion, he kissed them, and wept over them. At which the other Brothers marveled, and took some scandal that he, being a man of such great sanctity, should from mere human and worldly affection as it seemed, thus weep for his brother, and show more devotion to his remains than to those of the other Brothers, who had been of no less sanctity than Brother Humilitas, and were worthy of equal reverence.

And Brother Pacificus, knowing the untoward thoughts of the Brothers, humbly gave them the satisfaction they required, and said to them: "My dearest Brothers, be not surprised if I have done more for the bones of my own brother, than for the others; for, blessed be God! I was not moved thereto, as you believe, by human affection; but I did it, because when my brother departed this life, as I was praying in a deserted place and at a distance from him, I saw his soul ascend by a straight path to heaven; and therefore I am certain that his bones are sacred, and ought to be in paradise. And if God had given me the same certainty as to the other Brothers, I would have done the same reverence to their remains as to his." Then the Brothers, seeing his holy and pious intention, were well edified, and praised God, Who has done such marvelous things in His holy ones, the Brethren.

XLVII

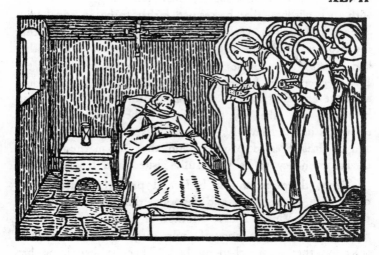

*OF the holy Brother to whom the Mother of Christ
appeared when he was sick, bringing him three
boxes of electuary.*

IN THE aforesaid House at Soffiano, there was in former
times a Friar Minor of so great sanctity and grace, that he
appeared totally transformed by Divine grace, and was continually ravished in God. On one occasion, as this Brother,
who was notably gifted with the grace of contemplation, was
wholly absorbed and lifted toward God, there came to him
birds of many different kinds, and familiarly perched on
his shoulders, and on his head, and on his arms, and his hands,
and all sang together marvelously. He loved to be alone,
and rarely would speak to anyone; but when he was asked

about any matter whatsoever, answered so graciously, and
with such wisdom, that he seemed rather to be an angel than
a man; and he was ever in prayer and contemplation; so that
the Brothers held him in great reverence. When this Brother
had finished the course of his holy life, according to the
Divine decrees, he became sick unto death, so that he could
not take anything either to eat or to drink; and besides this,
he would not take any medicine for the body, but all his
trust was in the heavenly Physician, Jesus Christ the Blessed,
and in His Blessed Mother; and thus he merited by the
Divine clemency to be mercifully visited and tended.

Being therefore in his bed, and preparing himself for
death with all his heart and devotion, there appeared to him
the glorious Virgin Mary, Mother of Christ, with a great
multitude of angels and of holy virgins, and with great
splendor, they approached his bed. Then he, beholding her,
took great comfort and joy both of soul and body; and
began humbly to pray, that she would intercede with her
beloved Son, that by His merits He would release him from
the prison of this miserable flesh. And as he persevered in
this petition, with many tears, the holy Virgin Mother
answered, calling him by name, and said to him: "Doubt
nothing, son, for thy prayer is heard, and I am come to comfort thee a little, before that thou depart from this life."
There were along with the Virgin Mother of Christ three
holy virgins, that carried in their hands three precious boxes,
filled with an electuary of surpassing fragrance and sweetness.
Then the glorious Virgin took one of the boxes, and opened
it, and the whole house was filled with sweet odors, and
taking thereof with a spoon, she gave to him that was sick;
and as soon as he had tasted it, he felt within himself such

comfort and such sweetness, that it seemed as though his soul could no longer remain within his body. Therefore he began to say: "No more, O most holy and blessed Virgin Mother, O blessed physician and saving refuge of mankind, no more; for I cannot sustain such sweetness!" But the benign and compassionate Mother continued to give him of the electuary, until the whole box was emptied.

Then having emptied the first box, the Blessed Virgin took the second, and put the spoon into it, to give him of that also; at which he cried out, saying: "O most Blessed Mother of God, my soul is almost melted away with the exceeding sweetness of the first heavenly food; how then can I sustain the second? I beseech thee, most blessed above all saints and angels, that thou give me no more." But the glorious Virgin Mary answered: "Taste, my son, yet a little more of this second box." And when she had given him a little thereof, she said: "Now, my son, it is enough; be comforted, for soon I will return for thee, and lead thee to the kingdom of my Son, which thou hast ever sought and desired." And having so said, she took leave of him, and departed, leaving him so fortified and consoled through the sweetness of this electuary, that he remained living for several days, strong and well, and without requiring any bodily nourishment. And after some days, whilst speaking joyfully with the Brothers, he passed with gladness and delight from this miserable life.

XLVIII

HOW Brother James of La Massa saw in a vision all the Friars Minor in the world, under the likeness of a tree.

Brother JAMES of La Massa, to whom God opened the door of His secrets, and gave the perfect knowledge and understanding of the Holy Scriptures and of future events, was endowed also with so great sanctity, that Brother Giles of Assisi and Brother Lucidus, and Brother Mark of Montino and Brother Juniper, said of him, that they knew of no one in this world so much after God's own heart as he. I also had a great desire to see him, because once when I was asking Brother John, a companion of the above-mentioned Brother Giles, to explain to me a certain matter in the spiritual life, he said to me: "If you would be well informed in the spiritual walk, seek to obtain an interview with Brother James of La Massa (because Brother Giles himself desired to be informed by him) and none can add aught to his words, nor take aught from them, for his mind has penetrated into the Divine secrets, and his words are the words of the Holy Spirit, and there is not a man upon earth with whom I myself desire so much to speak."

This Brother James, in the beginning of the ministry of Brother John of Parma, whilst praying one day, was ravished in God, and remained three days rapt in this ecstasy, all bodily sensation being suspended; and in such a state of insensibility, that the Brothers doubted if he were not dead. And while in this rapture, it was revealed to him by God what should hereafter come to pass within our Order; for which cause when I heard of it, I was the more desirous to hear him and to speak with him. And when it pleased God to give me the consolation of conversing with him, I entreated him thus: "If what I have heard of thee be true, I pray thee, keep it not hidden from me. I have heard that when thou wast as one dead for three days, God revealed to thee among other things what should befall our Order: this was reported to me by Brother Matthew, the Minister of the Marches, to whom thou didst reveal it by holy obedience." Then Brother James, with great humility, acknowledged that what Brother Matthew said was the truth.

And that which Brother Matthew told me was as follows: I knew a Brother, said he, to whom God has shown what shall hereafter befall our Order; for Brother James of La Massa revealed to me, that after many other things which God made known to him about the state of the Church

Militant, he was shown also in vision a tree, great and beautiful, the roots of which were all of gold and the fruits were men, and these men were all Friars Minor. The principal branches were distinct, according to the number of Provinces in the Order, and each branch bore as many Friars as there were severally belonging to the Province represented by that branch. And thus he knew the number of all the Brothers belonging to each Province, in the Order, and the names of them all, and the state and condition of each, and their offices and dignities, and the graces, and also the faults of each one of them. And he saw Brother John on the topmost branch, in the midst of all the others, and the Ministers of all the Provinces were at the top of the surrounding branches.

And after all this, he beheld Jesus Christ, seated on a great and shining throne, and He called St. Francis to Him, and gave him a chalice full of the spirit of life; and He sent him forth, saying: "Go, visit thy Brethren, and give them to drink of this chalice of the spirit of life; because Satan shall arise against them, and shall buffet them, and several of them shall fall, and shall not be able to recover themselves." And He gave him two angels to accompany him. Then St. Francis came and offered the chalice of life to all his Brothers: he began, offering it first to Brother John of Parma, who receiving it, drank it all fervently and with haste; and immediately he became all shining as the sun. And after him, St. Francis offered it to each of the other Brothers; but few of them received it with due reverence and devotion, or drank the whole of it. Those who received it devoutly and drank it all immediately became resplendent as the sun, and those who wasted it, and did not receive it with devotion, became black, or dark, and deformed and horrible to behold; whilst those who drank part, and in part wasted it, became partly shining and partly dark, and each more or less, according to the measure of their drinking, or wasting the cup. But more than all the others, the aforesaid Brother John shone resplendent, who had more perfectly drunk out the contents of the chalice of life, by which also he had looked more deeply into the abyss of the Infinite Light of Divinity; and thus he had foreseen the adversity and tempest which would arise against this tree, and toss and beat down its branches. Therefore he came down from the top of the branch where he was, and went down lower than all the branches, even to the bottom of the tree itself, where he remained hidden, and in a thoughtful mood.

And behold a Brother, who had drunk a part of the chalice and wasted the rest, climbed up the branch to the place whence Brother John had descended. And when he was seated thereon, the nails on his hands became sharp-cutting pieces of iron, as keen as razors: whereupon he quitted the branch whither he had climbed, and with great haste and fury would have thrown himself upon Brother John, to injure him. But Brother John seeing him coming, cried aloud, and commended himself to Christ, Who sat upon the throne; and at the voice of his crying, Christ called unto Him St. Francis, and gave him a sharp flint stone, and said to him: "Go, and with this stone cut off the nails of this Brother with which he would tear Brother John, so that he may not be able to hurt him." And St. Francis went and did as Christ had commanded him. And when he had so done, there came a tempest of wind, and shook the tree so violently, that the Brothers fell to the earth; and all those who had wasted the whole of the chalice fell first, and they were carried away by demons into dark and penal habitations. But Brother John, and the others who had drunk all the chalice, were translated by the angels, to the habitations of light, and of Life Eternal and beatific splendor.

And the aforesaid Brother James perceived and distinguished each one of them clearly, according to his name and condition and dignity. And so greatly did the wind blow against the tree that at the last it fell, and the wind carried it away. And immediately the storm ceased, there arose from the roots of this tree, which were of gold, another tree entirely of gold, producing golden leaves, and flowers, and fruits. Of this tree, and how it grew up, and took root downwards, and its beauty, its fragrance and its virtue, it is better to keep silence than to say more at this time.

XLIX

HOW *Jesus Christ appeared to Brother John of Alvernia.*

AMONG the other wise and holy Brothers and sons of St. Francis, who, as Solomon says, are the glory of their Father, there was in our own time, in the aforesaid Province of the Marches, the venerable and holy brother John of Fermo, who, on account of the length of time he had lived in the famous House of Alvernia, and because he passed away there from this life, was afterwards known as Brother John of Alvernia. The same was a man of great and singular holiness of life.

This Brother John, being as yet only a secular and a child, desired above all things the life of penance, which preserves the purity of the soul and of the body; so that even as a little child, he began to wear the iron heart and girdle on his flesh, and to use great abstinence. And especially whilst he abode with the Canons of St. Peter of Fermo, who lived in great splendor, he fled all carnal delights, and macerated his body with great rigidity of abstinence. But his companions in that place, being averse from this, took away from him his iron girdle, and hindered him in many ways from fasting; so that he bethought him, being inspired thereto by God, to leave the world with the lovers of it, and to cast himself entirely into the arms of Christ Crucified, in the habit of the crucified St. Francis: and so he did.

And being received into the Order whilst still but a child, and committed to the care of the Master of Novices, he grew so greatly in piety and in the spiritual life, that each time he heard the said Master speaking of God, his heart melted like wax approaching the fire. And with so much sweetness and grace was he enkindled by the Divine love, that he could not contain himself abiding in one place, but arose, and as one inebriated with the Spirit of God, ran to and fro about the garden, or the wood, or the church, according as the fire and impulses of the Holy Spirit led him. And thus in the process of time, Divine grace caused this angelic soul to grow continually from one degree of virtue to another, and in heavenly gifts, and divine elevation and ecstasies; so that his mind was lifted up — now to the splendors of the Cherubim, now to the ardor of the Seraphim, now to the joys of the Blessed, and even to the ecstatic and loving embraces of Jesus Christ. And especially on one occasion above others, the flame of Divine love so enkindled his heart, that for three years after, during which it continued to remain with him, he received unceasingly the most marvelous consolations and Divine visitations, and was constantly ravished in God; and in brief, during the whole time appeared to be all on fire, and glowing with the love of Christ; and this took place in the holy Mount of Alvernia.

But because God has a singular care of His children, giving them variously at one time consolations, at another tribulations, now prosperity, now adversity, according as He sees that they have need to be maintained in humility, or else to increase in them the desire of heavenly things; it pleased the Divine goodness, at the end of three years, to take away from the said Brother John the glow and fire of the Divine love, and to deprive him of all spiritual consolation. And thus Brother John, being left without the light and love of God, was altogether disconsolate and afflicted: for which cause, in the anguish of his heart, he now went to and fro in the wood, seeking to recall with his voice, and with tears and sighs, the Beloved Spouse of his soul, Who had departed and hidden Himself from him, and without Whose Presence his soul found no solace or repose. But nowhere and in no way could he find his sweet Jesus, nor return to that spiritual sweetness which he had tasted in the love of Christ aforetime. And this tribulation lasted many days; during which he persevered in continual weeping and sighing to entreat of God to restore to him one day, of His pity, the Beloved Spouse of his soul.

At last, when it had pleased God sufficiently to prove his patience and increase his desire, as Brother John was going as aforesaid through the wood, burdened and afflicted, he sat down, overcome with weariness, at the foot of a beech tree, and thus remained with his face all bathed in tears, looking up to heaven; and behold, suddenly Jesus Christ appeared to him, in the path by which he himself had come, and stood close by, but without speaking a word. Then Brother John seeing and knowing that it was the Lord, immediately cast himself at His feet, and with many tears, most humbly besought Him, saying: "Help me, O my Lord, who without Thee, most sweet Savior, am in darkness and mourning; without Thee, O most gentle Lamb of God, I am in anguish and in pain and fear; without Thee, O Son of God Most High, I remain in shame and confusion; without Thee, I am blind and deprived of all good; for Thou, Lord Jesus Christ, art the true Light of our souls; without Thee, I am lost and damned for ever, because Thou art the Life of our souls, and Life of life; without Thee, I am barren and withered, because Thou art the Fountain of grace, and of all good gifts; without Thee, I am altogether desolate, because Thou art Jesus our Redemption, our Love, and our Desire, the Bread of consolation, and Wine that rejoices the hearts of the angels and of all the saints. Enlighten me, most gracious Master and most tender Shepherd, for I am Thy little sheep, although unworthy so to be." But because the desire of His saints, when God delays to answer it, increases in them a greater love and a greater merit, Christ the Blessed departed without granting his prayer, and without answering him a word, by the same path by which He came.

Then Brother John arose, and ran after Him, and again threw himself at His feet, and with holy importunity held Him back, and with most fervent tears, said to Him: "O most sweet Lord Jesus Christ, have pity on my tribulation; hear me, through the multitude of Thy mercies, and by the truth of Thy salvation and restore to me the joy of Thy countenance, and look in pity on me, because the whole earth is full of Thy mercy." And yet again Christ departed, and neither spoke to him nor gave him any consolation; but did with him as a mother with her child, who, to make it the more desire the breast, lets it follow her crying, that it may take it the more willingly. Thus Brother John also followed Christ, with yet greater fervor and desire; and when he was come to Him, Christ the Blessed turned, and looked upon him with a serene and gracious countenance, and taking him in His most holy and merciful arms, He embraced him most tenderly. And as He thus opened His arms, Brother John saw issuing from the most Sacred Heart of the Savior rays of resplendent light, which illumined the whole wood, and himself also, in body and soul. Then Brother John knelt down at His feet, and the Blessed Jesus, as to a second Magdalene, graciously gave him His foot to kiss; and Brother John, holding it with all reverence, bathed it with so many tears that he appeared indeed another Magdalene, and said fervently: "I beseech Thee, my Lord, that Thou look not upon my sins, but by Thy most holy Passion, and by the sprinkling of Thy most Precious Blood, revive my soul in the grace of Thy love, seeing that this is the commandment that Thou hast given us, that we should love Thee with all our heart, and with all our affection; which commandment none can keep without Thy help. Help me then, O most beloved Son of God, that, according to Thy commandment, I may love Thee with all my heart and with all my strength."

And as Brother John prayed thus at the feet of Christ, his prayer was heard, and he received from Him the first grace, namely, the flame of Divine love, and felt himself entirely consoled and renewed. And knowing within himself that the gift of Divine grace was restored to him, he began to give thanks to the Blessed Christ, and devoutly to kiss His feet. And raising himself to see Christ face to face, Jesus Christ held out to him His most holy hands to kiss; and when Brother John had kissed them, he came nearer, and leant on the breast of Jesus, and kissed it and embraced Him; and Christ also kissed and embraced him. And whilst he did so, Brother John perceived so divine a fragrance, that if all sweet and fragrant odors of the world had been united in one, they would have seemed but as a stink in comparison with that odor; and thereby Brother John was ravished and consoled, and inwardly illuminated; and he retained this sweet fragrance in his soul many months.

And from that time forward his lips, which had drunk from the fountain of Divine wisdom at the Sacred Heart of Jesus, uttered marvelous and celestial words which moved all hearts, and brought forth great spiritual fruit in those that heard. And in that path in the woods, where the blessed feet of Christ had stood, and for a good distance around, Brother John always perceived the same fragrance, and saw the same resplendent light, when he passed that way, for long after. And returning to himself from his ecstasy, and the bodily Presence of Christ having vanished, his soul remained so inwardly illumined from the depths of His Divinity, that although he was a man unlearned in human knowledge, nevertheless he marvelously solved and explained the highest and most subtle questions, as to the Blessed Trinity, and the most profound mysteries of the Holy Scriptures. And often afterward he spoke before the Pope and the Cardinals, and to the king and his barons, and the masters and doctors, and all were astonished at the sublime words he spoke, and the profound judgments he gave to them.

L

HOW Brother John of Alvernia, as he said Mass on All Souls' Day, saw many souls delivered from purgatory.

As BROTHER JOHN was once saying Mass on the day after All Saints', for the souls of all the dead, as the Church has ordered, he offered the most august Sacrifice — which for its efficacy the holy souls desire more than all other benefits whatever that can be conferred upon them — with such fervent devotion and effectual charity, that he seemed as though entirely dissolved with the sweetness of his compassion and fraternal love. And thus as he devoutly elevated the Body of Christ, and offered it to God the Father, and prayed that for the love of His Blessed Son, Jesus Christ, Who hung upon the Cross for the redemption of our souls, it would please Him to deliver from the pains of purgatory the souls He had created and redeemed; immediately he beheld an innumerable multitude of souls ascend out of purgatory, like sparks of fire out of a burning furnace, and he saw them go up into heaven, through the merits of the Passion of Christ, which every day is offered for the living and the dead in this most holy Sacrifice, worthy to be adored through all eternity.

*OF Brother James of Fallerone; and how, after his
death, he appeared to Brother John of Alvernia.*

Brother JAMES of Fallerone, a man of great sanctity
of life, was dangerously ill once at the Community of Moliano,
which was in the Province of Fermo; and Brother John of
Alvernia, who loved him as a dear father, hearing of it,
betook himself to prayer, earnestly entreating God in his heart
to restore him to bodily health, if it was for the good of his
soul. And as he prayed thus fervently he was ravished in
ecstasy, and saw in the air above his cell, which was in the
wood, a great army of saints and angels, shining with such
splendor that all the country round was illumined by it;
and in the midst of the angels, he saw him for whom he

prayed, Brother James who was sick, arrayed in white and shining garments. He saw also among them the blessed Father St. Francis, adorned with the sacred Stigmas of Christ, and with great glory. Besides these, he recognized the holy Brother Lucidus, and Brother Matthew of Monte Rubbiano, and many other Brothers, whom he had never seen, or known in this life.

And as he looked with joy on this blessed multitude of saints, it was revealed to him that his Brother who was sick should die in this illness, and that for certain his soul should be saved; but that he should not enter paradise immediately on his death, because it behooved him first to be purified a little while in purgatory. This revelation gave Brother John such consolation, that for joy of the salvation of his Brother's soul he thought nothing more of the death of his body; but with the greatest inward sweetness he called him in spirit, saying: "Brother James, my sweet father; Brother James, my beloved Brother; Brother James, most faithful servant and friend of God; Brother James, companion of the angels, and fellow citizen of the saints!"

And in the joy of this certainty, he returned to himself, and immediately he departed from thence, and went to visit the said Brother James at Moliano; and found him so weighed down with sickness that hardly could he speak. Then he announced to him his approaching death, and the salvation and glory of his soul, according to the certainty, which had been given him by the Divine revelation, which Brother James received with a joyful heart and countenance, so that he laughed for mirth and gladness of his soul, thanking him for the good tidings he had brought, and devoutly commending himself to his prayers. Then Brother John besought him earnestly that he would return after his death, and tell him of his state; and this he promised to do, if it should please God. And having thus spoken, and the hour of his departure being near, Brother James began devoutly to recite the verse of the Psalm; *In pace in idipsum dormiam et requiescam;* which is to say, "I will sleep in peace, and rest in the Life Eternal"; and having said these words with a bright and joyful countenance, he passed away from this life.

And after his burial, Brother John returned to the House at La Massa, and waited for the promise of Brother James, that he would return to him on the day he had said. But on the said day, as he was praying, Christ appeared to him, with a great company of angels and saints, and Brother James was not among them; at which Brother John greatly marveling, recommended him fervently to Christ our Lord. The following day, as Brother John was praying in the wood, Brother James appeared to him, accompanied by angels, all shining and glorious; and Brother John said to him: "O Father most beloved, wherefore didst thou not come to me on the day promised?" And Brother John answered: "Because I had need of some purgation; but in the same hour when Christ appeared to thee, and thou didst commend me to Him, He heard thee, and delivered me from all pains. And immediately I appeared to Brother James of La Massa, that holy lay Brother who, as he served the Mass, beheld the Sacred Host, when the Priest elevated it, changed and transformed into the form of a fair and lovely Child; to whom I said: 'Behold I go with this Child to the kingdom of eternal life, without Whom none can enter there.'" And having said these words, Brother James disappeared, and went up to Heaven, with all the blessed company of the angels; and Brother John remained much consoled. Brother James of Fallerone died on the Vigil of St. James the Apostle, in the month of July, in the above-mentioned Community House of Moliano, where, after his death, many miracles were wrought through his merits by the Divine Goodness.

LII

OF the vision of Brother John of Alvernia, whereby
he understood all the order of the Holy Trinity.

THIS Brother John of Alvernia, because he had perfectly
stifled all worldly and temporal delights and consolations, and
had placed all his delight and all his hope in God, received
from the Divine Goodness marvelous consolations and revelations, especially on the Feasts of our Blessed Lord. Now once,
when the Feast of the Nativity of Christ was approaching —
when he confidently expected to receive special consolations
from God, in the sweet humility of Jesus — the Holy Spirit
put into his heart such an excessive and fervent love of the
charity of Christ, which caused Him to humble Himself so
far as to take upon Him our humanity, that it seemed to him
as though in very deed his soul was being drawn from his
body, and was burning like unto a furnace. And not being
able to sustain this inward fire, he was in anguish, and as
one wholly dissolved and melted away, and cried out with a
loud voice; and he could not restrain himself from crying out,
because of the impetuosity of the Holy Spirit, and the excessive fervor of his love. And in the same hour, as there came
to him this immeasurable fervor, there came to him also so
strong and certain a hope of salvation, that for nothing in the
world could he believe that, had he died then, he should have
had to pass through the pains of purgatory.

And this ardent love lasted over six months, although its
excessive fervor was not continual, but came to him at certain
hours of the day. And during this time, he received marvelous
visitations and consolations from God, and at divers times

he was rapt in ecstasy, as was seen by that Brother who first wrote of these things. Among other such times, one night he was so raised up and ravished in God, that he saw Him as the Creator of all things, and all created things in Him, both celestial and terrestrial, and all their several perfections, and grades and distinct orders. And then also he clearly perceived how all created things are present to their Creator, and how God is above, and within, and before and behind all His creatures. Afterwards he perceived God as One in Three Persons, and Three Persons in One only God; and the infinite charity which caused the Son of God to become incarnate, in obedience to His Father. And finally, in the vision, he perceived how that there is no other way by which the soul can go to God and have life eternal, but through Christ, the Blessed, Who is the Way, the Truth, and the Life of the soul.

LIII

HOW Brother John of Alvernia, as he was saying Mass, fell down as one dead.

To THE same Brother John of Alvernia, in the same Community House of Moliano, there befell once the following miraculous circumstance, as was related by the Brothers, who were present and saw it. On the first night after the octave of St. Lawrence, and within the octave of the Assumption of Our Lady, having said matins in the church with the other Brothers, and feeling within himself the unction of Divine grace coming upon him, he withdrew into the garden to contemplate the Passion of our Lord, and to dispose himself to celebrate Mass, which it was his turn to sing that morning. And thus as he was meditating on the words of consecration of the Body of Christ, and considering the infinite charity of Christ therein, Who would redeem us, not only with His Precious Blood, but by leaving us His adorable Body and Blood to be the food of our souls, he began to wax so full of fervor, and tenderness in the love of his sweet Jesus, that his soul could no longer contain itself for sweetness; and he cried aloud, and as though inebriated with the Holy Spirit, and ceased not to say: *Hoc est corpus meum.* Inasmuch as whilst saying these words, it seemed to him, that he saw Christ the Blessed, with His Virgin Mother, and a multitude of angels, and as he spoke to them, he was inwardly illumined by the Holy Spirit, as to the whole height and depth of the mysteries of the most august Sacrament.

And when the dawn was come, he entered the church under the same impression and with the same fervor of spirit, and still speaking the same words, not believing that he was either heard or seen by anyone; but there was a certain Brother in the choir who heard and saw all. And not being able to contain himself by reason of the abundance of the Divine grace, he cried with a loud voice, and continued to do so until it was time to say the Mass; when he went and prepared himself to go to the altar. And when he had begun the Mass, the further he proceeded, the more there grew within him the love of Christ, and the fervor of devotion, by which he received an ineffable impression of the Divinity, which he could neither explain to himself, nor express with his tongue. Therefore fearing that this fervor and this impression would increase so far that he should be obliged to discontinue the Mass, he was in great perplexity, and knew not which course to take, whether to proceed with the Mass, or to stand still, and wait.

But because on other occasions also the same thing had befallen him, and our Lord had so tempered this fervor that he had been enabled to finish his Mass, and trusting that it would be the same now as at other times, he went on with the Mass, though with great apprehension, and came as far as the Preface of our Lady, when the Divine illumination and the benign sweetness of the love of God began anew to grow within him with such force, that when he came to the *Qui pridie,* he could hardly sustain any longer such sweetness and delight. At last having come to the act of Consecration, and having pronounced the first half of the words over the Host, namely, *Hoc est enim* — by no means could he proceed any further, but continued only to repeat over again the same words. And the reason why he could go no further was, because he saw and felt the Presence of Christ amidst a multitude of angels, Whose majesty he was unable to sustain; and he saw also that our Lord did not enter the Host, nor the Host become changed into the Body of Christ, until he should be able to add the remaining half of the words, namely, *Corpus meum.*

Wherefore as he stood thus in his anxiety, and not proceeding any further, the Guardian and the other Brothers, and many seculars besides, who were in the Church hearing Mass, came round about the altar, and stood, looking on with astonishment, and watching the actions of Brother John, and many of them were weeping through devotion. At last, after a great while, when it pleased God, Brother John added the words *Corpus meum,* with a loud voice, and immediately the form of the bread disappeared, and in the place of the Host, there appeared Jesus Christ the Blessed, incarnate and glorified, and made known to him the humility and the charity which He manifested in becoming incarnate of the Virgin Mary, and which He manifests every day, in coming into the hands of the priest when he consecrates the Host: by which cause he was still more raised up in the sweetness of contemplation.

When he had elevated the Host and the consecrated Chalice, his soul was ravished, so that he became unconscious, and all sensation being suspended, his body fell backwards, and if he had not been supported by the Guardian, who stood behind him, he would have fallen to the ground. Wherefore the Brothers running to him, and the seculars also who were in the Church, both men and women, carried him into the sacristy, as one dead, for his body was cold, and his fingers were clenched so tightly that it was hardly possible to unclose or to move them. And he remained in this ecstasy as one half dead until the hour of terce. It was in the summer time.

I, who was present also, desiring much to know what God had wrought in him, as soon as he had come to himself went to him, and prayed him, for the love of God, to tell me all that had taken place; and he, because he much confided in me, related the whole to me in order; and among other things, he told me that whilst he was considering the Body and Blood of Jesus Christ there present, his heart melted like wax in a great heat, and it seemed to him as though his flesh was without bones, so that scarcely could he lift his arms, or his hands to make the sign of the Cross on the Host or the Chalice. And again he told me that before he was made a priest it was revealed to him by God that he should swoon in the Mass, but because he had said many Masses without this happening, he thought that the revelation was not from God. Nevertheless, about fifty days before the Assumption

of our Lady, when this thing at last befell him, it was again
revealed to him by God, that this should be the case during
the Feast of the Assumption: but that afterward, he had no
recollection of this vision, nor of the revelation made to him
by our Lord.

OF THE MOST HOLY
STIGMATA OF ST. FRANCIS

OF THE MOST HOLY
STIGMATA OF ST. FRANCIS

I

The First Consideration on the Holy Stigmata.

ST. FRANCIS being arrived at the age of forty-three years, in the year 1224 was inspired of God to leave the Valley of Spoleto, and to go into Romagna, with Brother Leo, his companion. And as they went, they passed by the foot of the castle of Montefeltro, in which castle there was at that time assembled a great company and procession, on account of one of the Counts of Montefeltro being newly knighted. And St. Francis hearing of this solemnity, and that there were there assembled many nobles and gentlemen from divers countries, said to Brother Leo; "Let us go to this festival; perhaps, with the help of God, we may produce good spiritual fruit there." Among the other nobles of the country, who had come to this count, was one, a great and wealthy gentleman of Tuscany, who was named Orlando da Chiusi, of Casentino; who, for the wonders which he had heard concerning the sanctity of St. Francis, and the miracles worked by him, had a great veneration for him, and a great desire to see him, and to hear him preach. St. Francis, therefore, arriving at the castle, entered therein and went to the courtyard among the multitude of nobles and gentlemen assembled; and in fervor of spirit he mounted upon a parapet, and began to preach, taking for the text of his sermon these words, in the common language of the people: "So great is the good that I hope for, that all pain delights me." And on this theme he discoursed, by the dictation of the Holy Spirit, so fervently and pro-

foundly, citing the divers pains and sufferings of the holy
Apostles and holy martyrs, and the severe penances of holy
confessors, and the manifold tribulations and temptations of
holy Virgins and other saints, that all the people stood, with
their eyes and their minds turned towards him, and listened
as if an angel of God spoke.

Among the rest, the aforesaid Orlando, touched to the
heart by God through the marvelous preaching of St. Francis,
determined in his mind to confer with him after the sermon,
and take counsel on the affairs of his soul. Therefore, the
sermon being ended, he took St. Francis aside, and said to
him: "O Father, I would converse with thee about the salvation of my soul." St. Francis replied: :"Most willingly; but
go first and do honor to thy friends, who have invited thee to
the feast, and dine with them; and after the dinner, we will
talk as much as thou wilt." Orlando therefore went to
dinner, and after dining, he returned to St. Francis and conversed with him, and laid before him fully the state of his
soul. And finally, this Orlando said to St. Francis: "I have
in Tuscany a mountain, called the Mount of Alvernia, a
place most solitary, and as it would seem most holy, exactly
suited to anyone who desired to do penance in a place remote
from all men, or to live a life of solitude; and if it please
thee, I will willingly give it to thee and thy companions, for
the salvation of my soul." St. Francis, hearing this generous
offer of that which he greatly desired, rejoiced exceedingly;
and praised and thanked God first, and then Orlando, and
said thus to him: "Orlando, when thou hast returned to thy
house, I will send to thee some of my companions, and do
thou show them this mountain; and if it appear to them suited
for a place of penance and prayer, I will at that same hour ac-

cept thy charitable offer." And having said this, St. Francis departed: and having completed his journey, he returned to St. Mary of the Angels; and likewise Orlando, after the festivities of the court were over, returned to his castle, which was called Chiusi, and was a mile only from Alvernia.

St. Francis, therefore, having returned to St. Mary of the Angels, sent two of his companions to Orlando: and when they were come to him, he received them with very great joy and charity. And wishing to show them the mountain of Alvernia, he sent with them fifty armed men to defend them against the wild beasts of the forest; and he himself accompanied the Brothers, and they ascended the mountain, and diligently explored it. At last they came to a part of the mountain, most suited for devotion and for a place of contemplation, where also there was a plain; and this spot they chose for their habitation and that of St. Francis. And with the help of the armed men who accompanied them, they made cells with the branches of trees; and thus they accepted the gift in the Name of God, and took possession of the mountain of Alvernia, and of the habitation of the Brothers therein. And they departed, and returned to St. Francis.

And when they were come to him, they told him how and in what way they had taken possession of a place on the mountain of Alvernia, specially suited to prayer and to contemplation. Hearing these tidings, St. Francis rejoiced greatly and praised and thanked God, and spoke to the Brothers, with a joyful countenance, saying: "My sons, we are approaching our Lenten Fast of St. Michael the Archangel; I firmly believe that it is the will of God we should pass this Lent on the Mount Alvernia, on which by Divine Providence a place has been prepared for us, that to the honor and glory of God and His glorious Virgin Mother Mary, and of the holy angels, we may, through penance, merit to receive from Christ the consolation of consecrating this blessed mountain." And having said this, St. Francis took with him Brother Masseo da Marignano of Assisi, who was a man of great judgment and great eloquence; and Brother Angelo Tancredi da Rieti, a man of high and noble birth, who had been a knight whilst in the world; and Brother Leo, a man of the greatest simplicity and purity, for which cause St. Francis loved him much. And with these three Brothers, St. Francis betook himself to prayer, recommending himself and the said three Brothers to the prayers of those who remained, and set out with these three in the name of Jesus Christ crucified, to go to Mount Alvernia.

And as they went, St. Francis called to him one of his three companions, Brother Masseo, and said thus to him: "Thou, Brother Masseo, shalt be our Guardian and our Superior in this journey, whilst we are going and staying together, and we will observe one rule, that we may either be saying the Office, or speaking of God, or keeping silence, and not thinking either of eating or drinking or sleeping; but when it is time to put up for the night, we will beg a little bread, and remain and rest there, where God shall provide for us." Then these three companions inclined their heads, and made the sign of the Cross, and went on their way: and the first evening they came to a House of the Friars and lodged there. The second evening, because of the bad weather, and because they could not reach any house belonging to the Brothers, nor any other house or castle, they took refuge from the weather in a deserted and ruined church, and there lay down to rest. And when his companions slept, St.

Francis betook himself to prayer; and behold, in the first watch of the night, there came a great multitude of ferocious demons, with great noise and violence, and began vehemently to attack and to torment him; one laid hold upon him on this side and one on that; one pulled him up and another pulled him down: one threatened him with one thing and one reproved him with another, in order to distract him in his prayer: but they could not, because God was with him.

Therefore when St. Francis had sufficiently borne the assaults of the demons, he began to cry with a loud voice: "O damned spirits, you can do nothing but what the hand of God permits; and in the Name of Almighty God I say to you, do unto my body whatever is permitted you by God; know that I will bear it willingly, because I have no greater enemy than my body; and therefore if you avenge me of my enemy, you will do me a great service."

Then the demons with the greatest impetuosity and fury took him and began to tear and to drag him about the church, and to make more disturbance and do him more harm than at the first. And St. Francis cried out and said: "My Lord Jesus Christ, I give Thee thanks for so much honor and charity, which Thou dost unto me; for this is a sign of great love, when the Lord punishes well His servant for all his defects in this world, for then he shall not be punished in the next. And I am ready to sustain joyfully all pains and all adversities, which Thou, my God, willest to send me for my sins." Then the demons, confused and vanquished by his constancy and patience, departed.

And St. Francis in fervor of spirit went out of the church, and went into a wood which was near, and gave himself to prayer, and with supplication and tears and beating of his breast, sought to find Jesus Christ, the spouse and delight of his soul. And finding Him at last in the secret depth of his soul, he now spoke to Him reverently as his Lord; now answered Him as his Judge; now besought Him as his Father; now conversed with Him as with a friend.

On this night and in this wood, his companions, who had come out after him and remained to observe and to watch what he did, saw and heard him, with tears and supplications, entreat the Divine Mercy for sinners. He was then seen and heard weeping with a loud voice over the Passion of Christ, as though he saw it before him, with his bodily eyes. In this selfsame night, they saw him praying with his arms stretched out in the form of a cross, and for a great space suspended and elevated above the earth, surrounded by a resplendent cloud. And thus, in such holy exercises, he passed the whole night without sleep.

And in the morning his companions, knowing that through the fatigues of the night, which he had passed without sleep, St. Francis was feeble in his body, and might take harm if he went on foot, they went to a poor peasant, and begged him, for the love of God, to lend his ass for Brother Francis, their Father, who could not go on foot. Hearing the name of Brother Francis, the man said: "Are you of the Brethren of that Brother Francis of Assisi, of whom so much good is spoken?" The Brothers answered: "Yes, and that it was indeed for him that they had begged the ass." Then the good man, with great devotion and solicitude, got ready the ass, and led him to St. Francis, and with great reverence helped him to mount and to proceed on his journey; and he went with them, walking behind his ass.

And when they had gone some way, the peasant said to St. Francis: "Tell me, art thou Brother Francis of Assisi?" And St. Francis answered, "Yes." "Try then," said the peasant, "to be as good as all think thee to be, because many have great faith in thee; and therefore I admonish thee to be nothing less than people hope of thee." St. Francis, hearing these words, disdained not to be admonished by a peasant, nor said within himself, "How coarse and ignorant is he who admonishes!" but he immediately dismounted and threw himself on the ground, and knelt before the man and kissed his feet; and thanked him humbly for having condescended to admonish him so charitably. Then the peasant, along with the companions of St. Francis, with great reverence lifted him from the ground and replaced him on the ass, and journeyed further.

And when they had gone about half-way up the mountain, the peasant began to be very thirsty, because the heat was great, and the ascent fatiguing, and presently began to cry behind St. Francis, saying: "Woe's me, how I pant for thirst! if I do not get something to drink, I shall quickly be choked." For which cause St. Francis descended from the ass, and prostrated himself in prayer; and he remained on his knees and with his hands lifted up to Heaven, until he knew by revelation that God had heard him. And St. Francis said to the peasant: "Run quickly to yonder stone, and thou shalt find there living water, the living water which Jesus Christ by His mercy, at this hour, has caused to flow from this stone." The man ran to the place which St. Francis had shown him, and found a beautiful spring which sprang from the hard rock by virtue of the prayer of St. Francis, and he drank copiously and was comforted. And it was well seen that this fountain was miraculously produced by God at the prayer of St. Francis, because neither before nor since was there ever a fountain of water in that place, nor any running water anywhere near, nor for a great space around. This done, St. Francis, with his companions and the peasant, returned thanks to God for the miracle He had shown them, and journeyed farther.

And as they approached the foot of the rocks belonging to Alvernia, it pleased St. Francis to rest awhile beneath the shade of the oak by the wayside, which is there to this day, and from under it he began to consider the lay of the country, and of the place they were going to. And while he considered, there came a great multitude of birds from all parts, which, with singing and beating of their wings, all showed the greatest joy and gladness, and surrounded St. Francis in such manner, that some perched on his head, some on his shoulders, some on his arms and some on his legs, and some around his feet. His companions and the peasant, seeing this and marveling, St. Francis, all joyful in his spirit, said to them: "I believe, most beloved Brothers, that it pleases our Lord Jesus Christ that we should inhabit this solitary mountain, because so much joy is shown at our arrival by our little sisters and brothers, the birds." And saying thus, they arose and journeyed further, and at last came to the place which their companions had chosen beforehand.

II

The Second Consideration on the Holy Stigmata.

ORLANDO, hearing that St. Francis, with three companions, was about to ascend the mountain to take possession of it, was filled with joy. And the next day he set out with many people of his castle to visit them, taking with him bread and wine and other things needful for them. And when he arrived at the summit, he found them all in prayer; and approaching, he saluted them. Then St. Francis, turning to him with the greatest benignity and joy, welcomed both him and his people, after which they sat down and conversed together.

And after they had talked awhile, and St. Francis had returned thanks to him for the holy mountain which he had given them, and for his coming to them, St. Francis requested him also that he would build him a little cell at the foot of a beautiful beech tree which was distant about a stone's throw from the place where the Brothers were lodged, because it seemed to him a spot most apt and set apart for prayer. And Orlando immediately caused it to be built as St. Francis had said. And this done, because the evening was now approaching and it was time to go, St. Francis preached to them in a few words before they departed; and after he had preached and given them his blessing, Orlando took him and his companions aside, and said to them: "My dearest Brothers, I would not have you suffer any bodily want in this wild mountain, by which you might be less able to attend to spiritual things; and therefore I desire, and this I say to you once for all, that you will confidently send to my house for whatever you need; and if you do otherwise, it will give me very great pain." And having said thus, he departed with his people, and returned to his castle.

Then St. Francis made his companions sit down, and instructed them as to what manner of life they must lead, they and all those who would lead religious and solitary lives.

And amongst other things, he exhorted them especially to the observance of holy Poverty, saying: "Do not regard so much the charitable offer of Orlando, as that you in no way offend against our Lady and Mistress, holy Poverty. Know of a surety, that the more we shun Poverty, the more the world will shun us, and the more we shall suffer need; but if we closely embrace holy Poverty, the world will come after us, and will provide for us abundantly. God, Who has called us into holy Religion for the salvation of the world, has made this compact between us and the world, that we are to give the world good example, and the world is to provide for our necessities. Let us therefore persevere in holy Poverty, because this is the way of perfection, and the earnest pledge of eternal riches." And after many holy and beautiful words and instructions on these matters, he concluded by saying: "This is the mode of life which I impose on myself and on you; and because I see myself to be near the time of my death, I purpose to remain in solitude, and alone with God, to weep before Him over my sins: and Brother Leo, when it seems good to him, can bring me a little bread and water; but on no account suffer any secular to come to me, but answer for me to all that come." And having said these words, he gave them his blessing, and went his way to his cell by the beech tree; and his companions remained in the same place, with the firm resolution to observe his commands.

And after some days, as St. Francis was standing by his cell considering the conformation of the mountain, and marveling at the immense fissures and apertures in the great rocks, it was revealed to him by God, while he prayed, that these mighty chasms had been miraculously opened in the hour of the Passion of our Lord, when, as the Evangelist relates, the rocks were rent asunder. And it was the will of God that this should more particularly take place in this mountain of Alvernia, because the Passion of our Lord Jesus Christ should there be renewed in the soul of St. Francis by loving compassion, and in his body by the sacred Stigmata.

Having received this intimation, he immediately shut himself up in his cell, and retired wholly into himself, to await the mystery that should be revealed. And from this time forward, he began, through the unceasingness of his prayer, to taste more frequently the sweetness of Divine contemplation, through which oftentimes he was rapt in God, so that his companions saw him raised bodily above the ground, and completely ravished out of himself. In these contemplative raptures there were revealed to him by God not only things present and future, but even the secret thoughts and desires of the Brothers: as Brother Leo, his companion, experienced within himself in those days.

This Brother Leo being assailed by the devil with a very great temptation, not of a carnal but of a spiritual nature, had a great desire to have something pious written by the hand of St. Francis, and thought if he had it the temptation would leave him, either wholly or in part: but through shame and reverence, he had not the courage to speak of this desire to St. Francis. But that which Brother Leo did not tell him was revealed to him by the Holy Spirit. Wherefore St. Francis called him, and bade him fetch paper and pen and ink; and with his own hand inscribed the praise of Jesus Christ, signing it with the letter *Tau** and gave it to him saying: "Take,

---

*St. Jerome, commenting on Ezechiel 9, says that in his time the letter *Tau*, which is the last letter of the Hebrew alphabet, was used in the Samaritan language to represent the Cross, of which it had the form.

most beloved Brother, this paper, and keep it diligently until thy death. May God bless thee, and keep thee against every temptation. And be not downcast because thou art tempted; for the more thou art assailed by temptation, the more I repute thee the servant and friend of God and the more I love thee. Verily, I say to thee, that none should esteem himself perfectly the friend of God, except in so far as he has passed through many temptations and tribulations." And Brother Leo, receiving this writing with all faith and devotion, immediately all the temptation departed from him; and returning to the place where they lodged, he related to his companions with great joy the grace which he had received from God through this writing of St. Francis; and preserving and keeping it diligently, the Brothers afterwards worked many miracles by means of it.

And from that hour, the same Brother Leo began, with great purity of good intention, to observe slowly and to consider the life of St. Francis; and by reason of his purity, he merited to see him again and again ravished in God, and suspended above the earth, sometimes to a height of three, sometimes to a height of four cubits, and sometimes as high as the top of the beech tree; and sometimes he saw him raised so high above the earth, and surrounded with such splendor, that scarcely could he see him at all. And what should this simple Brother do, when St. Francis was elevated from the ground only a little way, so that he could reach him? He went softly to him, embraced his feet, and kissed them with tears, saying: "My God, have mercy on me a sinner, and, through the merits of this holy man, give me to find grace with Thee." And on one such occasion, standing thus beneath the feet of St. Francis, when he was raised so far above the earth that he could not touch him, he saw a scroll, written in letters of gold, descend from heaven, and rest on the breast of St. Francis, and on the scroll were written these words: *Here is the grace of God;* and when he had read it he saw it return into heaven.

By the gift of this grace of God, which was in him, St. Francis was not only ravished in Divine ecstatic contemplation, but also on several occasions comforted by angelic visitations. Thus, as he was one day thinking of his death, and of the state of his Order after his life should be ended, and saying: "Lord, my God, what will become after my death of this Thy poor little family, which of Thy benign goodness Thou hast committed to me a sinner? who will comfort them? who will correct them? who will pray to Thee for them?" and other such words, there appeared to him an angel sent from God, and comforted him, saying thus: "I declare to thee on the part of God, that the profession of thine Order shall never fail until the Day of Judgment, and there will never be so great a sinner but that if he love thine Order from his heart, he shall find mercy with God, and none who persecute thine Order through malice shall live a long life. Moreover, no wicked person within the Order, if he amend not his life, shall long remain in it. And therefore, grieve not thyself if thou see in thine Order certain Brothers not good for much, who observe not the Rule as they ought, nor think that for this the Order shall decline; for there shall always be in it a great multitude who will follow perfectly the evangelical life of the Gospel of Christ and the purity of the Rule; and then, immediately after the death of the body, shall enter into life eternal, without passing through any purgatory; others will follow it, but not perfectly, and these, before they enter paradise, shall suffer purgatory, but the time of their purgation shall be committed to thyself by God. But as for those who do not observe the Rules at all, regard them not, for God Himself doth not regard them." And the angel having said these words departed, and St. Francis remained comforted and consoled.

After this, as the Feast of the Assumption of our Lady was approaching, St. Francis sought opportunity to lodge more solitarily and secretly, that so he might the more privately keep the Forty Days' Fast of St. Michael, which begins with the Feast of the Assumption. And he called Brother Leo to him, and spoke thus: "Go and stand in the doorway of the Oratory, where the Brothers are lodged, and when I call thee, return to me." Brother Leo went therefore, and stood at the door; and St. Francis waited a little, and called aloud. Then Brother Leo hearing him call, returned to him; and St. Francis said to him: "My son, let us seek another more retired spot, where thou canst not hear me when I call." And seeking further, they found at some distance, on the southern side of the mountain, a solitary spot exactly suited to his desire: but it was impossible to get to it, because there lay an immense rock with a yawning and fearful chasm in front of it. But with great pains, they laid a piece of wood across it, so as to form a bridge, and got over.

Then St. Francis sent for the other Brothers, and told them how it was his intention to pass the Forty Days' Fast of St. Michael in this solitary spot; and he prayed them to make him a little cell there, where no cry of his could be heard by them. And when the cell was made, he said to them: "Go ye to your place, and leave me alone, for I purpose, with the help of God, to keep the Fast undisturbed, and without distraction of mind, and therefore, let not any of you come to me, nor suffer any one to come. But thou only, Brother Leo, and once only in the day, come to me with a little bread and water, and once again in the night at the hour of matins; and then come silently, and when thou art at the end of the bridge, thou shalt say: *Domine, labia mea aperies:* if I answer thee, pass over, and come to the cell, but if I answer thee not, then depart quickly." And St. Francis said thus, because several times he had been so ravished in God, that he had neither heard anything, nor felt any bodily sensation. And having thus spoken, he gave them his blessing, and they returned to their place.

And the Feast of the Assumption being now come, St. Francis began to keep the Fast with very great abstinence and austerity, macerating his body, and comforting his spirit with fervent prayer, vigil, and discipline; and in these his prayers, he grew continually from grace to grace, disposing his soul to receive the Divine mysteries and the Divine splendors, and his body to sustain the cruel assaults of the demons, with whom many a time he had bodily conflicts. And among others it happened once during this Fast that St. Francis, coming one day out of his cell, and betaking himself fervently to prayer in the hollow of a cleft rock, from whence a fearful precipice descended from an immense height to the ground, the devil suddenly appeared to him under a terrible form, with a very great tempest, and tumult, and struck him, in order to thrust him down the precipice. Then St. Francis, having nowhere to fly, and not able to endure the hideous aspect of the demon, turned quickly back, and sought with hands and feet and with all his body to cling to the rock, recommending himself to God and feeling about with his hands for something to hold on to. But as it pleased God, Who never suffers His servants to be tempted above what they are able to bear, the rock to which he was clinging immediately hollowed itself into the shape of his body and received him into itself, so that he sank into it as though it had been melted wax, imprinting the form of his hands and face on the rock: and thus, by the help of God, he escaped from the devil.

But that which the evil spirit could not do at that time to St. Francis, he did a good while after his death to one of his dear and holy Brothers, who was carrying some pieces of wood to the same place, in order to make it possible to visit it without peril, out of devotion to St. Francis and the miracle which had there taken place. One day the devil pushed him with violence, when he had a large log on his head which he was going to lay across the chasm, and caused him to fall down, with the log still upon his head. But God, Who had concealed and preserved St. Francis from falling, by his merits concealed and preserved the Brother also from the peril of his fall for, as he fell, he commended himself with a loud voice and with great devotion to St. Francis, who immediately appeared to him, and took him and placed him gently down at the foot of the rocks, without his having sustained the least shake or bruise. Now the Brothers who had heard him cry out as he fell, believed that he must be dead, considering the great height from which he had fallen and the sharpness of the rocks beneath him; and they took a bier, and, with great sorrow and weeping, came from the other side of the mountain, with intent to gather up the fragments of his body, and to bury them. And when they had descended the mountain, the Brother who had fallen came to meet them, with the same log on his head with which he had fallen, and singing *Te Deum laudamus* with a loud voice. And as they greatly marveled, he related to them in order all the manner of his fall, and how St. Francis had rescued him from all peril. Then all the Brothers went with him to the spot, devoutly singing *Te Deum laudamus,* and praising and thanking God and St. Francis for the miracle which had been performed for their Brother.

Now in the aforesaid Forty Days' Fast, St. Francis, as had been already told, although he sustained many attacks from the demons, yet nevertheless received much consolation from God, not only through angelic visitations, but through the birds of the wood. For during all the time of the Fast, a falcon, which had built its nest close to the cell, woke him every night a little before matins with its note, and with the beating of its wings against the cell, and departed not until he arose to say matins; and when he happened to be more weary than usual, or weak and infirm, the falcon, like a discreet and compassionate person, woke him later than usual. And for this cause St. Francis took great delight in this bird, because by its solicitude for him it drove from him all idleness, constantly inviting him to prayer; and besides this, oftentimes by day it would sit familiarly with him.

St. Francis, being greatly weakened in body through his great abstinence and the assaults of the demons, and desiring to sustain his body by the spiritual nourishment of the soul, began to think upon the immeasurable glory and joy of the Blessed in the Life Eternal: and to pray that God would grant him the favor of tasting a little of this joy. And as he thought thus within himself, suddenly there appeared to him an angel in great splendor, who had a viol in his left hand, and in his right hand a bow; and whilst St. Francis stood stupefied at the vision the angel drew the bow once across the viol, and immediately there was heard such sweet melody that his soul was inebriated with sweetness, and he lost all bodily sense: insomuch that, as he afterwards related to his companions, he thought that, if the angel had drawn the bow a second time across the strings, his soul, through excessive sweetness, would have parted from his body.

III

The Third Consideration on the Holy Stigmata.

IT CAME to pass, at the approach of the Feast of the most holy Cross, in the middle of September that Brother Leo went one night to the usual place, and at the usual hour, to say matins with St. Francis. And calling from the top of the bridge, according to custom, *Domine labia mea aperis,* and St. Francis not responding, Brother Leo did not go back as St. Francis had commanded him, but with a good and holy intention passed over the bridge, and went softly into his cell, and not finding him there, thought he had gone to some place in the wood to pray. Wherefore he went out again, and by the light of the moon, went softly searching through the wood: and at last he heard the voice of St. Francis, and approaching him, he saw him on his knees in prayer, with his face and his hands raised to heaven: and heard him say, in fervor of spirit, "Who art Thou, O my most sweet God? and what am I, most vile worm, and Thy worthless servant?" And these same words, he repeated continually, and said nothing besides.

At which Brother Leo, marveling, raised his eyes, looking up to heaven; and as he looked, he saw coming from heaven a torch of fire, most resplendent and beautiful, which descended and rested on the head of St. Francis; and from this flame he heard a voice issue forth which spoke with St. Francis, but Brother Leo could not understand the words. Hearing this voice, and judging himself unworthy to stay so near the holy ground when this wonderful apparition was taking place, and fearing besides to offend St. Francis or to trouble him in his contemplation, if he should perceive his presence, he withdrew softly into the background, and standing afar off, waited to see the end. And looking fixedly, he saw St. Francis extend his hands three times to the flame; and finally, after a great space of time, he saw the flame return to heaven. After this he departed securely, and glad at heart at the vision he had seen, and returned toward his cell.

But as he went thus, secure in his own mind, St. Francis perceived him by the rustling of the leaves under his feet, and commanded him to wait for him, and not to move. Then Brother Leo obediently stood still and waited, with such fear that, as he afterwards told his companions, at that moment he would rather the earth should swallow him up than wait for St. Francis, as he thought he would be displeased with him; because he was wont with all diligence to guard himself against offending his Father, lest for his fault St. Francis should deprive him of his company.

Then St. Francis coming to him, asked: "Who art thou?" And he all trembling, replied: "I am Brother Leo, my Father." And St. Francis said to him: "Wherefore hast thou come here, Brother Little Sheep? Have not I told thee not to come and observe me? Tell me by holy obedience, if thou hast seen or heard aught?" Brother Leo answered: "Father, I heard thee say several times: 'Who art Thou, O my most sweet God? who am I most vile worm, and Thy worthless servant?'" And then kneeling down before St. Francis, Brother Leo confessed the fault of disobedience which he had committed against his command, and implored his pardon with many tears. And afterwards he prayed him earnestly to expound to him the words he had heard, and to declare to him those which he had not understood.

Then St. Francis, seeing that God had revealed this to the humble Brother Leo, and that He had indeed permitted him for his simplicity and piety to hear and to see so much, condescended to reveal and to explain to him that which he had asked, saying; "Know, Brother Little Sheep of Jesus Christ, that when I said these words which thou heardest, there was shown to me in my soul two lights; one of the understanding of myself, the other the knowledge of the Creator. When I said: 'Who art Thou, O my most sweet God?' then I was in that light of contemplation in which I saw the depths of the infinity of the goodness and wisdom and power of God; and when I said 'What am I?' I was in that light of contemplation, in which I saw the profound deplorableness of my own vileness and misery; and then I said; 'Who art Thou, Lord of infinite goodness and wisdom, Who dost deign to visit me, who am a vile and abominable worm?' And in that flame which thou sawest was God, Who spoke to me in this manner, as He spoke of old to Moses. And among other things which He said to me, He asked of me that I should give Him three gifts; and I answered Him: 'My Lord, I am all Thine; thou knowest that I have nought but my tunic and my cord, and even these things are Thine; what then can I offer and give to Thy Majesty?' Then God said to me: 'Seek in thy bosom, and offer Me what thou shalt find there.' I sought therefore therein, and found a ball of gold; and I offered it to God; and thus I did three times, according as God three times commanded me; and then I knelt down thrice and blessed and thanked God, Who had given me something to offer Him. And immediately it was given me to understand that these three offerings signified holy obedience, uttermost poverty, and resplendent chastity, which God by His grace has given me to observe so perfectly, that in nothing my conscience reproves me. And as thou didst see me put my hand in my bosom, and offer to God these three virtues, signified by the three balls of gold which God had placed there, thus has God given me virtue in my soul, that for all the benefits and all the graces which His most holy goodness has bestowed on me, I should ever with my heart and my mouth praise and magnify Him. These are the words which thou heardest when thou sawest me lift up my hands three times. But take heed to thyself, Brother Little Sheep, that thou watch me no more, and return to thy cell with the blessing of God, and have a care for me: because in a few days God will do such great things on this mountain, that all the world will wonder; for He will do some new thing, which He has never yet done to any creature in this world."

And having said these words, he had the Book of the Gospel brought to him, because God had put it into his soul that after three times opening the Book of the Gospel, it should be shown to him what it would please God to do with him. And the book being brought to him, St. Francis prostrated himself in prayer. His prayer being finished, he had the book opened three times by the hand of Brother Leo, in the Name of the Most Holy Trinity; and as it pleased the Divine Providence, in each of these three times there always appeared the Passion of Christ. By this thing it was given him to understand, that, as he had followed Christ in the acts of His life, so he must follow Him and be conformed to Him in His afflictions and sorrows, and in His Passion, before he should pass out of this life. And from this time forward, St. Francis began to taste and to feel more abundantly the sweetness of Divine contemplation, and of the Divine visitations, by one of which he had an immediate preparation for the impression of the most holy Stigmata; and in this wise.

The day before the Feast of the most holy Cross, in the middle of September, St. Francis being secretly in prayer within his cell, an angel of God appeared to him, and said to him on the part of God, "I have come to comfort thee, and to admonish thee that thou prepare and dispose thyself humbly and with all patience to receive that which God shall give to thee, and work in thee." St. Francis replied: "I am ready to receive patiently everything that it pleases my Lord to do unto me." And when he had said thus, the angel departed.

The next day being come, namely, the Feast of the most holy Cross, St. Francis prostrated himself betimes in prayer before the opening of his cell, and inclined with his face towards the east, according to his wont, praying thus: "O my Lord Jesus Christ, I pray Thee to grant me two graces before I die; the first, that in my lifetime I may feel in my soul and in my body, so far as is possible, all the pain and grief, which Thou, O sweet Lord, didst feel in Thy most bitter Passion; the second, that I may feel in my heart, so

far as is possible, that excessive love by which Thou, the Son
of God, wert impelled willingly to sustain so great sufferings
for sinners." And he remained a long time thus in prayer,
trusting that God would grant him what he asked, and that,
as far as it was possible for a mere creature, it should be
permitted to him to feel these things, as he had said.

Then, having received this promise, St. Francis began to
contemplate with the deepest devotion the Passion of Christ
and His infinite charity. And being inflamed by this contemplation, on this same morning, he saw coming from heaven
a seraph with six fiery and resplendent wings, and approaching
him with great speed, so that he could discern him clearly,
and know certainly, that he had the form of a man crucified;
and that his wings were so disposed, that two extended themselves above his head, two stretched themselves in the act of
flight, and two covered his whole body. Seeing this, St. Francis
was much afraid, and filled at one and the same time with joy
and grief and admiration. He had the greatest joy at seeing
the gracious aspect of Christ, Who appeared to him so
familiarly, and looked upon him so graciously; but on the
other hand, seeing Him nailed to the Cross, he had immeasurable grief and compassion. At the same time he marveled
much at this stupendous and unwonted vision, knowing well
that the infirmity of the Passion did not agree with the im-
mortality of the seraphic spirit. And being in this amazement,
it was revealed to him, by the seraphic spirit, that by Divine
Providence the vision was shown to him in this form, because
God intended that by the inflaming of his mind, and not by
corporal martyrdom, he should be wholly transformed into the
express similitude of Christ Crucified through this admirable
apparition.

The whole mountain of Alvernia then appeared burning with resplendent flame, which shone forth and illumined all the mountain and the valleys around, as though the sun were risen upon the earth; so that the shepherds who were watching their flocks in that country, seeing all the mountain as it were on fire, and so great light around it, had the greatest fear, as they afterwards related to the Brothers, affirming that this illumination remained upon the mountain of Alvernia for the space of an hour or more. In like manner owing to the splendor of this light, which shone through the windows of the hostelries of the country round, certain muleteers who were going into Romagna rose with haste, believing that it came from the rising of the sun, and saddled and loaded their beasts; and as they journeyed along, they saw the light cease, and the natural sun rise.

After the said seraphic apparition, Christ, Who then appeared to him, spoke to St. Francis certain high and secret things which he would not reveal during his lifetime to anyone; but after his life was ended, he revealed them, as will be shown further on; and these were His words: "Knowest thou what I have done unto thee? I have given thee the Stigmata, which are the signs of My Passion, because thou shalt be My ambassador. And even as I, on the day of My death, descended into limbo, and delivered all the souls I found there by virtue of My wounds, so also do I grant to thee that every year, on the anniversary of thy death, thou shalt go to purgatory, and all the souls thou shalt find there of thy three Orders, namely, of the Friars Minor, of the Sisters and Virgins, and of the others also, who shall have remained sincerely devoted to thee, thou shalt deliver by virtue of these thy Stigmata, and shalt lead them into the glories of paradise, that so thou mayest be conformed to Me in thy death, as thou hast been in thy life."

Then this wonderful vision disappeared, after a great space of time and of secret converse, leaving in the heart of St. Francis an excessive ardor and flame of Divine love, and in his flesh a marvelous image of and resemblance to the Passion of Christ. For in his hands and feet there immediately began to appear the marks of the nails, in the same manner as he had seen them in the flesh of Jesus Christ Crucified, Who had appeared to him under the form of the seraph, so that his hands and feet appeared to be pierced through the middle with nails, the heads of which were in the palms of his hands and the soles of his feet; and the points came out again in the back of the hands and the feet, and were turned back and clinched, in such manner that within the bend formed by the reversal of the points a finger could easily be placed, as in a ring; and the heads of the nails were round and black. Similarly in his right side there was the appearance of a wound made by a lance, not healed, but red and bleeding, which many times ran with blood from the holy heart of St. Francis, and stained his tunic and his nether garments. Whence his companions, before they knew it from himself, perceiving that he never uncovered his hands nor his feet, and that he could not put the soles of his feet to the ground, and afterwards finding his tunic and other garments stained with blood when they washed them, understood with certainty that in his hands and feet, and also in his side, he bore the exact image and similitude of our Lord Jesus Christ Crucified. And whilst he exerted himself to the uttermost to hide and to conceal those sacred and glorious Stigmata, so clearly impressed in his flesh, and on the other hand, found that he could hardly conceal

them from his familiar companions, fearing to publish the
secrets of God, he was nevertheless in great doubt whether he
ought to reveal the seraphic vision, and the impression of the
most holy Stigmata.

Finally, incited thereto by his conscience, he called to him
all his most familiar companions, and propounded to them his
doubt, in general words and without explaining to them the
fact, asking their counsel. Among these Brothers there was
one of great sanctity, named Brother Illuminato. He, being
truly illumined of God, understood that St. Francis must have
seen something marvelous, and answered him: "Brother Francis,
know, that not for thyself alone, but also for others, God has
shown thee on several occasions His hidden mysteries; and
therefore thou hast reason to fear lest, if thou keep concealed
what God has shown thee for the benefit of others, thou
shouldst be worthy of censure." Then St. Francis, moved by
his words, with great fear related to them all the mode and
the form of the aforesaid vision; adding that Christ, Who had
appeared to him, had spoken to him certain things, which he
would never tell so long as he lived. And although those most
holy wounds, inasmuch as they had been impressed on him by
Christ Himself, gave the greatest joy to his heart; nevertheless
in his flesh and to his bodily sensation, they gave intolerable
pain. Whence, constrained by necessity, he chose Brother Leo
among all the others, as the most simple and most pure, to
whom he revealed all, and let him see and touch those holy
wounds, and bind them with handkerchiefs to mitigate the
pain and to receive the blood, which issued and dropped from
them; which bandages, in time of sickness, he let him change
frequently, even every day, except from Friday evening to
Saturday morning; because during that time in which our

Lord Jesus Christ was crucified for us, died and was buried, he would not allow the pains of the Passion of Christ, which he bore in his body, to be mitigated for him by any human remedy or medicine. And it happened several times, when Brother Leo was removing the bandages from the wounds, that St. Francis through the pain which it gave him to have them torn off put his hands on the breast of Brother Leo, who by the touch of those holy hands felt such sweetness of devotion in his heart, that he nearly fell to the ground.

St. Francis, having completed the Fast of St. Michael the Archangel, soon after disposed himself by Divine revelation to return to St. Mary of the Angels. Therefore he called to him Brother Masseo and Brother Angelo, and, after many words of farewell and of holy instruction, he commended to them with all the earnestness he could the care of that holy mountain, saying that as for Brother Leo and himself, it behooved them to return to St. Mary of the Angels. And having thus said, he was accompanied by them a part of the way, and blessed them all, in the Name of Jesus Crucified. And yielding to their prayers, he gave them his holy hands, adorned with those glorious and sacred Stigmata, to see and touch, and to kiss; and so leaving them comforted, he departed from them, and descended from the holy mountain.

IV

The Fourth Consideration on the Holy Stigmata.

WE HAVE now to relate how St. Francis, having completed the Forty Days' Fast in honor of St. Michael on the holy mountain of Alvernia, descended the mount with Brother

Leo and with a devout peasant, on whose ass also he rode, because that for the nails in his feet, he could not well put them to the ground. When he had come down, therefore, from the mountain — the fame of his sanctity having spread through the country, and the shepherds having declared how they had seen the whole mountain of Alvernia lit up and in flames, and that this must be the sign of some great miracle God had worked in him — as soon as the people of the country heard that he was passing, all of them made haste to see him, both men and women, great and small; and all of them with the greatest devotion and desire sought to touch and kiss his hands. And not being able to escape the devotion of the people, although the palms of his hands were wrapped in bandages he concealed them also beneath the sleeves of the habit, the more to hide the secrets of God, and only allowed his fingers to be seen and kissed. But for all his pains to hide the sacred mystery of the holy Stigmata, in order to fly the occasion of earthly glory, it pleased God, for His own glory, to show forth many miracles by virtue of them; and most especially during this journey from Alvernia to St. Mary of the Angels, as well as many more afterward, in divers parts of the world, both during his life and after his glorious death; in order that by these clear and evident miracles the hidden and marvelous virtue of the most holy Stigmata, and the excessive charity and mercy of Christ, so wonderfully shown in his regard, might be manifested to the world; and of these we will only relate the following.

One day, as he approached a village on the confines of the district of Arezzo, a woman came to meet him, shedding many tears, and carrying her son in her arms, who had suffered from dropsy for eight years, ever since he was four years of age, and whose body was so enlarged, that when he stood upright, he could not see his feet. And she set him down before St. Francis, and besought him to entreat God for him. Then St. Francis first of all betook himself to prayer; and his prayer being ended, he placed his holy hands on the body of the child, and immediately the swelling disappeared, and he was perfectly healed. And he restored him to his mother, who received him with the greatest joy, and led him back to the house, returning thanks to God and St. Francis, and willingly showing her little son, now restored to health, to all who dwelt in that country and came to her house to see him.

On the same day St. Francis passed through the borough of St. Sepulchre, and as he approached the castle, the inhabitants of the town and of the country round went forth to meet him, and many of them went before him with branches of olive in their hands, crying aloud: "Here is the Saint! Here is the Saint!" And through the devotion of the people and the desire that they had to touch him, there was a great throng, and they pressed upon him. But he, going his way, with his mind elevated and ravished in God through contemplation, although the people touched him and held him and pulled him, passed on like one insensible, knowing nothing of what was going on around him, neither what was said or done, never aware that he was passing near the castle, or through that country. And when he had passed through the town, and the people had returned to their homes, he came to a leper house, about a mile beyond the town. And returning to himself, as one coming back from another world, the heavenly contemplative asked his companions: "When shall we be getting near the town?" Thus truly his soul fixed and ravished in the contemplation of heavenly things, had no consciousness of the things of earth, nor of change of place nor of time, nor of those who went by. And this was often the case, as his companions by direct experience clearly perceived.

The same evening, they arrived at the Community House of Monte Casale, where was a sick Brother so cruelly and horribly tormented by his illness, that it seemed rather as though it were some infliction and torment of the devil, than natural infirmity; for often he would fling himself down on the earth, trembling violently and foaming at the mouth; and sometimes there would come a twitching of all the nerves of his body; and, the muscles would stretch, bend, writhe, and turn, until his heels were drawn up to the nape of his neck, and then he would leap up in the air, and immediately fall down again. And as St. Francis was at table, he heard from the Brothers of the miserable and incurable state of their companion, and being moved with compassion he took a slice of bread that he was eating and made the sign of the most holy Cross thereon with his holy hands that had the sacred Stigmata, and sent it to the sick Brother, who, as soon as he had eaten it, was perfectly cured, and never more felt aught of his infirmity.

And the next morning having come, he sent two Brothers, who were of that House, to Alvernia, that they might stay there, and with them he sent back the peasant who had come along with his ass which they had borrowed, desiring that he should return in their company to his home. And after remaining a few days longer in the same House, he departed, and went on to the city of Castello. And behold, many of the townsfolk came to meet him, bringing with them a woman that a long time was possessed of the devil, and humbly prayed him for her deliverance; because by her doleful howling and barking like a dog, and piercing shrieks, she disturbed the whole country round. Then St. Francis, having first prayed and made on her the sign of the most holy Cross, commanded the devil to come out of her; and immediately he departed from her, leaving her sound in mind and body. And she having told this miracle to all the people, behold another woman, with great faith, brought him her child, who was dangerously ill with a cruel wound in his body, and fervently besought him to make the holy sign on it with his hands. Then St. Francis in answer to her devotion, took the child, and removed the bandages from his wound, making the sign of the most holy Cross three times upon it, and then, with his own hands, replaced the bandages and gave him back to his mother. And because it was evening, she put him immediately to bed that he might sleep. And in the morning, when she went to get him up, she found the bandages gone; and looking upon him, she saw that he was perfectly healed as though he had never ailed aught, except that where the wound had been, the flesh had grown together, like to a crimson rose; and this rather in testimony to the miracle than as a result of the wound; for this same rose remained with him all his life long, and produced in him a special devotion to St. Francis every time he looked upon it.

In this town St. Francis sojourned for a month, at the entreaty of the devout citizens, during which time he performed many more miracles; and after this, he departed and went on his way to St. Mary of the Angels with Brother Leo, and with a good man who had lent him another ass on which he rode. And it came to pass that because of the bad roads and the inclement weather, though they journeyed on all day, they could not reach the house where they were to remain the night; therefore, constrained by the darkness and the storm, they took shelter for the night which was coming on, and from the snow which was beginning to fall, in a hollow cave in the rock. And as they lay thus, with much inconvenience and badly covered, the good man to whom the ass belonged could not sleep for the cold; and as there was no means of making a fire, he began to complain bitterly within himself, and to lament and murmur against St. Francis, who had led him into such a place. Then St. Francis, perceiving this, had compassion on him; and in the fervor of his charity, put out his hand, and touched him on his; when behold, a new wonder! immediately he touched him with that hand which was seared and pierced with the fire of the seraph, the cold completely vanished; and such a warmth entered into the man, as it seemed to him both from before and behind, that it was as though he were near to the mouth of a burning furnace. And feeling himself entirely comforted in body and in soul, he fell asleep until the morning; and more sweetly, according to his own account, did he sleep there that night, among rocks and snow, than ever in his own bed.

On the following day they journeyed on again, and reached St. Mary of the Angels. And when they had come near unto it, Brother Leo lifted up his eyes, and looked towards the House, and saw a most beautiful cross, and on it the form of the Crucified, going before St. Francis, and in such a manner that, as he followed after it, when he went on, it went on, and when he stayed, it stayed; and such was the splendor and brightness of this cross, that not only did the face of St. Francis shine with it, but also all the way before and behind them was illumined by it; and it disappeared only as they entered the House of St. Mary of the Angels. Then

St. Francis and Brother Leo were received by the Brothers with exceeding great joy and fraternal charity; and from that time, St. Francis spent the most of his days in the House of St. Mary of the Angels until the day of his death. And the fame of his sanctity and of his miracles spread continually more and more throughout the Order and throughout the world, although in his profound humility he concealed, as well as he could, the grace and the gift of God, calling himself the greatest of sinners.

St. Francis, seeing that through the Stigmata his bodily strength grew less and less, so that he could no longer undertake the care of the Order, summoned the General Chapter; and when it was assembled, he humbly excused himself before his Brethren for his inability to continue to have the oversight of the Order, in so far as to fulfill the office of General; not that he entirely renounced the office, because having been made General by the Pope, he could not give up his office, or substitute a successor, without the Pope's express permission; but he chose for his Vicar, Brother Pietro Cattani, commending the care of the Order to him, and to the Ministers of the Provinces, with all the affection that he could. And having done this, he was comforted in spirit, and raised his hand and his eyes to heaven, and said: "To Thee, O Lord my God, to Thee I commend Thy family, which Thou hast committed unto me until this hour when by reason of my infirmity, which Thou knowest, O my sweetest Lord, I can no longer sustain the care of it. I commend it also to the Ministers of the Provinces; they shall answer for it at the Day of Judgment, if any Brother, by their negligence, or by their bad example, or their too harsh correction, should perish." And through these words, it pleased God that all the Brothers assembled together should understand that he spoke of the holy Stigmata, when he excused himself on account of his infirmity; and for the great devotion that they felt, none of them could refrain from weeping. And from this time forth he left all the care of the government of the Order in the hands of his Vicar and of the Ministers of the Provinces; and said: "Now that I have given up the charge of the Order on account of my infirmity, I have henceforth nothing more to do but to pray for it, and to give a good example to the Brothers. And I know of a truth that even if my infirmity were to depart, the greatest help that I could give to the Order would be to pray to God continually for it, that He would defend and govern and preserve it."

Now, as has already been said, although St. Francis was ingenious in hiding as much as possible the most holy Stigmata, and ever since he had received them went always with his hands bandaged and his feet covered, he was not able to prevent many Brothers from seeing and touching them in divers manners, and more especially the wound in his side, which he tried with the greatest diligence to conceal. Thus a Brother who was serving him induced him one day by a pious strategy to take off his tunic, that he might shake the dust out of it. And whilst St. Francis did so, as he stood by, he saw plainly the wound in his side; and putting his hand quickly on his breast he touched the wound with his three fingers, and measured its depth and breadth; and after a similar manner, his Vicar, Pietro Cattani, saw it also.

But Brother Ruffino saw it, and was assured of it, more plainly still. He was a man of the most profound contemplation; on which account St. Francis said of him more than once, that there was not in the whole world a man more holy than he; and on account of his sanctity, St. Francis loved him with an intimate affection, and let him do in all as he would. This Brother Ruffino assured himself in three distinct ways among others of the most holy Stigmata, and especially of that in the side. The first was, that having to wash the nether garments which St. Francis wore large enough to be drawn over the wound in the right side, so as to cover it, he examined and considered them attentively, and each time found them covered with blood on the right side; by which he knew certainly that the blood continued to flow from the wound; and for this, St. Francis reproved him, when he saw that he pryed into the garments which he laid off, in order to discover this sign. The second manner that the said Brother Ruffino employed was, that with great care one day he thrust his fingers into the wound, at which St. Francis, for the pain he felt, cried out: "God forgive thee, Brother Ruffino, that thou hast done this unto me!" The third manner was, that with great instance he besought St. Francis one day, as the greatest favor, to give him his cloak and take his instead, for the love of charity. And the Father full of charity consenting, although unwillingly, and taking off his cloak, gave it to him, and received his in its place, and during this taking off and changing of habits, Brother Ruffino plainly saw the wound.

In like manner Brother Leo and many other Brothers saw these sacred Stigmata of St. Francis during his lifetime: which Brothers — although on account of their sanctity they were worthy of belief on their simple word, yet to prevent all possibility of doubt — took their oath on the holy Gospels as to what they had clearly seen. Several Cardinals also, who were intimate with him, saw the holy Stigmata, and wrote pious and

eloquent hymns, antiphons, and proses on them. And Pope
Alexander himself, preaching on one occasion to a large
audience, where all the Cardinals were present, and among
others the holy Brother Bonaventure, said and affirmed that
he had seen with his own eyes the sacred Stigmata of St.
Francis, during his lifetime. And the Lady Jacopa di Settesoli
of Rome, who was the first lady of her time in Rome, and most
devoted to St. Francis, saw them, and kissed them several
times with great reverence, both before and after his death;
for which cause she came from Rome to Assisi by Divine
revelation to be present at his death, which happened in this
manner.

A few days before he died, St. Francis was taken ill at
Assisi, in the Palace of the Bishop, where he was staying
with several of his companions, and notwithstanding all his
sickness, he sang continually the praises of Jesus Christ. Now,
on a certain day, one of his companions said to him: "Father,
thou knowest that the citizens here have great faith in thee,
and hold thee to be a holy man; wherefore they may think
that if thou art what they think thee to be, thou shouldst
begin in this sickness to think of thy death, and rather weep
than sing, inasmuch as thy sickness is very grave. And know
that thy singing and ours, as thou wilt have us join in, is
heard by many, both in the palace and outside; because this
palace is guarded, on thy account, by many armed men, who
might take bad example from what thou doest; it seems to
me thou wouldst do well to depart from here, and let us all
return to St. Mary of the Angels, for we are not in our
place here amongst seculars." Then St. Francis answered him:
"My beloved Brother, thou knowest how two years ago, when
we were at Foligno, God revealed to thee, and afterwards also

to me, the time of my death, according to which in a few
days my life must end in this sickness: and in the same revelation God gave me the assurance of the remission of all my sins,
and of an entrance into the bliss of paradise. Before this
revelation was given me, I wept at the thought of death and
of my sins, but ever since I am so full of joy that it is
impossible for me to weep, and therefore I sing and will sing
to God, Who has given me the treasure of His grace, and
made me certain of the eternal treasure of the glory of
paradise. As to our departing from here, I consent and am
well pleased at it; only do thou find means of conveying me,
for because of my sickness I can no longer walk." Then the
Brothers took him up in their arms and carried him away,
accompanied by many of the citizens.

And when they had come near a hospice, which stood by
the way, St. Francis said to them that carried him: "Let me
down on the ground, and turn my face towards the city."
And when it was done, so that he looked toward Assisi, he
blessed it with many blessings, saying: "Blessed be thou of
God, O holy City, because by thee shall many souls be saved,
and in thee many servants of God shall dwell, and from out
of thee shall many be elected to the Kingdom of Eternal Life."
And having said these words he had himself carried on to St.
Mary of the Angels.

And when they had arrived, they carried him into the
infirmary, and laid him down to rest. Then St. Francis called
to him one of his companions, and said: "My beloved Brother,
God has revealed to me, that in this sickness, after a few days,
I shall pass away from this life; and thou knowest that the
Lady Jacopa di Settesoli, who is so greatly devoted to our
Order, if she heard of my death, and was not present at it,

would have overmuch sorrow; therefore send her word, that if she would see me alive, she should come at once." To which the Brother replied: "True, Father; and indeed, for the great devotion she has for thee, it would ill beseem that she should not be here at thy death." "Go therefore," said St. Francis, "and bring me ink, pen and paper, and write as I shall tell thee."

And when he had brought them, St. Francis dictated the letter to him thus: "To the Lady Jacopa, servant of God, Brother Francis, the poor little one of Christ, salutation and fellowship of the Holy Spirit and of our Lord Jesus Christ. Know, beloved, that Christ the Blessed has revealed to me by His grace, that the end of my life is at hand. And therefore if thou wouldst still find me alive, as soon as thou shalt receive this letter, arise and come to St. Mary of the Angels; because if thou come not speedily thou wilt not find me here: and bring with thee a shroud to wrap my body in, and the wax which will be needed for my burial. I pray thee also to bring me some of that food which thou wert wont to give me when I was sick at Rome." And when this letter was written, it was revealed to St. Francis from God that the Lady Jacopa was on her way to him, and was already near to the House, and that she had brought with her all those things which he had asked in the letter. Therefore he told the Brother who wrote it, to write no further, for there was no need, and to keep back the letter; at which the Brother marveled that he should not finish the letter, and dispatch it. And while he waited a little space, there came a loud knocking at the door, and St. Francis sent the porter to open it: and behold there stood at the door the Lady Jacopa, the noblest lady in Rome, with her two sons, Roman senators, and a great company of men on horseback; and entering, the Lady Jacopa went straight to St. Francis in the infirmary. At this meeting, St. Francis had great joy and consolation, and so had the lady also, seeing him alive and able to speak. Then she recounted to him that, being still in Rome, God had revealed to her whilst she was at prayer the speedy termination of his life, and that he would ask of her those things which she had brought with her. And she had them carried in to St. Francis, and persuaded him that he should eat.

And when he had eaten, and was much refreshed, the Lady Jacopa knelt down at his feet, and embracing those most holy feet, sealed and adorned with the wounds of Jesus Christ, she kissed them, and bathed them with her tears, with such excess of devotion that the Brothers thought verily they beheld the Magdalene at the feet of Christ, and by no means whatever could they draw her away. At last, after a great while, they raised her, and drew her aside; and asked of her how she had arrived so opportunely, and brought with her all those things which were needful to St. Francis, both for the remaining space of his life, and for his burial. Then the Lady Jacopa told them how that one night in Rome, whilst she was praying, she heard a voice from heaven, which said: "If thou wouldst see St. Francis alive, go without delay, and take with thee those things thou hast given him before when he was sick, and those things also which will be needed for his burial"; and, she said: "I have done so." And she remained there until St. Francis had passed from this life, and was buried. And at his burial she, with all her company, paid him the greatest honors, and at her own expense. And returning to Rome, within a little time after, this noble lady died a holy death; and out of her devotion to St. Francis, directed that she should be carried to St. Mary of the Angels, and buried there; and so it was done.

After the death of St. Francis, not only did the Lady Jacopa see and kiss his glorious sacred Stigmata, but many citizens of Assisi also did the same; and among them a certain cavalier, a great man and of great renown named Jeronimo, who had much doubted and was incredulous concerning them, even as St. Thomas the Apostle doubted of those of Christ Himself. And in order to assure himself and others, he ventured, in the presence of the Brothers and many seculars, to move about the nails in the hands and feet, and to feel the depth of the wound in the side. After which trial, he bore testimony to the fact, swearing on the Gospels that so it was, and that he had seen and touched them. St. Clare also, and her Religious, being present at his burial, saw and kissed the glorious sacred Stigmata of St. Francis.

V

The Fifth Consideration on the Holy Stigmata.

THIS last consideration contains certain visions and miracles which God wrought and manifested after the death of St. Francis, for the confirmation of his having received the most holy Stigmata, and in order to fix the day and the hour in which he received them from Christ.

And in the first place it must be related, how in the year of our Lord 1282, in the month of October, Brother Philip, Minister of Tuscany, by command of Brother John Buonagrazia, the Minister General, required under holy obedience

of Brother Matthew of Castiglione, a man of great devotion
and sanctity, that he should tell what he knew of the day
and the hour when the most holy Stigmata of Christ were
impressed on the body of St. Francis, as it was known that
he had had revelations concerning it. The same Brother
Matthew, constrained by holy obedience, replied in this
manner: "When I was in the community of Alvernia last
year, in the month of May, I was praying in the cell, where it
is believed the seraphic apparition took place. And in my
prayer, I earnestly begged of God that it would please Him
to reveal to some one, the day and the hour, and the place,
in which the most holy Stigmata were impressed on the body
of St. Francis. And as I persevered in this prayer, until after
the first watch of the night, St. Francis appeared to me in a
very great light, and said to me: 'Son, for what dost thou
ask God?' And I answered him: 'Father, I have asked for
such and such things.' And he said to me: 'I am Francis,
thy Father, dost thou know me well?' 'Father,' said I to him,
'I do.'

"Then he showed me the sacred Stigmata in his hands
and feet and side, and said: 'The time has come when God
wills, for His great glory, to manifest what hitherto the
Brothers have not bestirred themselves to inquire into. Know
then, that He who appeared to me was not an angel, but
Jesus Christ Himself under the form of a seraph, Who impressed with His own hands on my body these very wounds,
such as He had received them in His own Body on the Cross;
and it was in this wise: The day before that on which is kept
the Exaltation of the Holy Cross, an angel came to me, and
told me on the part of God, that I should prepare myself

with patience to receive that which God would send to me. And I answered that I was ready to receive and to endure whatever it should please God to send. Then the next morning, which was the morning of the Feast of the Holy Cross, and which that year fell on a Friday, I came out of my cell at dawn in great fervor of spirit, and betook myself to prayer in the place where thou now art, in which place I often prayed. And as I prayed, behold there descended through the air from heaven, with great impetus, a young man crucified, in the form of a seraph with six wings. At this marvelous sight I knelt down humbly, and began to contemplate with devotion the immeasurable love of Jesus Christ Crucified and the immeasurable pain of His Passion: and the sight of Him produced in me such a great compassion, that it seemed to me as though I felt His very Passion in my own body; and at His presence, all this mountain became resplendent as the sun; and He descended and came close to me. And standing before me, He spoke to me certain secret words, which as yet I have revealed to none; but the time is near when they shall be revealed. Then after a little space, Christ departed from me, and returned into heaven: and I found myself marked with these wounds. Go therefore,' said St. Francis, 'and assure thy Minister of these things, because this is the work of God, and not of man.' And having said these words, St. Francis blessed me and returned to heaven with a great multitude of youths in shining raiment." All these things the said Brother Matthew declared he had heard and seen, not sleeping, but waking. And afterward he took a solemn oath that he had told these things, under holy obedience, to the said Minister in his cell at Florence.

HOW a holy Brother prayed God that he might know the secret words spoken by the seraph, and how St. Francis himself revealed these words to him.

ON another occasion, a devout and holy Brother whilst reading the Legend of St. Francis, in the chapter where is related the history of the sacred Stigmata, began to think, with great anxiety of spirit, what might be the words concerning those secret things which the seraph spoke to St. Francis when he appeared to him, and which St. Francis had said he would never reveal to anyone as long as he lived. And thus the Brother said within himself: "These words St. Francis would not repeat to anyone during his lifetime; but after the death of his body perhaps he might relate them, if he were devoutly asked to do so." And from that time the devout Brother began to pray to God and St. Francis, that it would please them to reveal these words; and having persevered eight years in this prayer, in the eighth year he merited to have it answered; and in this wise.

One day, after they had dined and returned thanks in the church, he remained praying in another part of the church by himself; and as he prayed to God and St. Francis for this cause, with more than his usual fervor and with many tears, another Brother called him, and commanded him, on the part of the Guardian, to accompany him to the fields for the affairs of the house. At which, not doubting but that obedience is more meritorious than prayer, immediately he had heard the command of the Superior, he humbly left off praying, and went with the Brother who had called him; and as it pleased God, by this act of prompt obedience he merited that which by his protracted praying he had not obtained. For now as they both went out the door of the House, they met two strange Friars, who appeared to have come from a far country; one of them seemed to be young, and the other old and emaciated, and both of them, through the bad weather, were wet through and covered with mud. Wherefore this obedient Brother had great compassion for them, and said to the Brother whom he was accompanying: "Oh beloved Brother, would that the business on which we are going could be delayed a little, for these strange Brothers have great need to be charitably received. I pray thee let me go first and wash their feet, and especially the feet of the aged Brother, who has the greatest need, and do thou wash those of the younger, and afterwards we can go on the business of the Convent." Then the other Brother consenting to the charity of his companion, they returned to the Convent, and received these strange Brothers with great charity, and led them to the fire in the kitchen, that they might warm and dry themselves; where also eight Brothers belonging to the House were warming themselves.

And when they had sat awhile by the fire they led them apart to wash their feet, as they had agreed to do. And as the obedient Brother was washing the feet of the elder of the two, and removing the mud with which they were covered, he looked and saw that they were marked with the most holy Stigmata; and immediately, with joy and wonder he devoutly embraced them, and cried out: "Either thou art Christ, or thou art St. Francis!" At the sound of his voice and of these words, all the Brothers who were by the fire arose and came with haste, and beheld with great fear and trembling those glorious Stigmata. Then the aged Brother, at their entreaty, suffered the Friars to see them clearly, to touch and to kiss them. And as they wondered yet more and more, and were filled with joy, he said to them: "Doubt not, and do not fear, most beloved Brothers and my sons; I am your Father, Brother Francis, who, by the will of God founded three Orders. And because I have been entreated these eight years by this Brother who has just washed my feet, and today more fervently than at other times, that I would reveal to him the secret words which the seraph spoke to me when he gave me the Stigmata, which words I never would reveal in my lifetime, today, by the commandment of God, for the sake of his perseverance and of his prompt obedience by which he has given up the sweetness of contemplation, I am sent by God to reveal to you what he has asked."

And turning to the said Friars, St. Francis said thus: "Know, most beloved Brothers, that being on the mountain of Alvernia, wholly absorbed in the contemplation of the Passion of Christ, in that seraphic vision, I was thus stigmatized in my own body by Christ Himself; and He said to me: 'Knowest thou what I have done to thee? I have given thee the marks of My Passion, that thou mayest be My standard-bearer. And as I, on the day of My death, descended into limbo, and by virtue of My Stigmata, liberated all the souls I found there, and conducted them to paradise; so also I grant thee in this hour, in order that thou mayest be conformed to Me in thy death, even as thou hast been in thy life, that when thou shalt have passed away from this life, every year, on the anniversary of thy death, thou shalt go into purgatory, and by virtue of these Stigmata which I have given thee, shalt liberate all the souls thou shalt find there belonging to thy three Orders, Friars Minor, Sisters and Virgins, and over and above these, all who have been devout to thee, and shalt lead them to paradise.' These words of Christ I never revealed whilst I lived in this world." And having thus spoken, St. Francis and his companion suddenly disappeared. And many Brothers afterwards heard these things from the eight Brothers who were present during the vision, and had heard the words of St. Francis.

HOW St. Francis after his death appeared to Brother John of Alvernia.

ST. FRANCIS appeared on another occasion on Mount Alvernia to Brother John of Alvernia, a man of great sanctity, whilst he was in prayer, and spoke with him for a long time. And at last, as he was about to depart, he said to him: "Ask of me what thou wilt." And Brother John said: "Father, I pray thee that thou wouldst tell me what I have desired to know for a long time, where thou wert and what thou wert doing when the seraph appeared to thee." Then St. Francis answered: "I was praying in that place where stands the chapel of Count Simon of Battifolle, and asked two graces of my Lord Jesus Christ; the first was, that He would grant me in this life to feel in my soul and in my body, so far as possible, all the pains that He Himself felt, during the time of His bitter Passion. The second grace which I asked of Him was like unto the first, that I might feel in my heart the excessive love which induced Him to suffer such a Passion for us sinners. And then God put it into my heart, that He would give me to feel both the one and the other, in so far as it was possible for a mere creature; which thing indeed was fulfilled in me by the impression of the Stigmata."

Brother John asked him again, if the secret words which the seraph had spoken to him were such as had been related by the holy Brother aforesaid, who affirmed that he had so heard them from St. Francis in the presence of eight Brothers? And St. Francis replied, that this was the truth, as the Brother had said. Then Brother John, taking courage through this general condescension to his requests, said: "O Father, I beseech thee let me see and kiss thy most holy and glorious Stigmata, not that I doubt of aught, but solely for my consolation, and because I have always so greatly desired this favor." And St. Francis with good will showed them and presented them to him, so that he both clearly saw and touched, and also kissed them.

And finally, Brother John asked: "Father, what consolation didst thou not feel in thy soul, when thou didst see Christ the Blessed coming to thee to give thee the marks of His most Sacred Passion? Would to God that I might feel a little of the sweetness thereof!" And St. Francis answered: "Seest thou these nails?" Brother John said: "Yes, Father." "Touch, once again," said St. Francis, "this nail in my hand." Then Brother John with great reverence and fear touched the nail, and as soon as he had touched it, there came forth so great a fragrance, like to a cloud of incense, that, entering by his nostrils, it filled his soul and his body with such sweetness that immediately he was ravished in ecstasy and became insensible, and thus, he remained, rapt in God, from the hour of terce, when this took place, until vespers. And Brother John never spoke of this vision and familiar conversation with St. Francis except to his confessor, until he came to die; when, being near to death, he revealed it to several of the Brothers.

HOW a holy Brother saw a wonderful vision concerning one of his companions who was dead.

IN THE Province of Rome there was a certain holy and devout Brother, who saw the following wonderful vision. One of the best beloved companions among the Brothers, having died in the night, was buried on the following morning, at the entrance to the choir. And on the same day this Brother withdrew himself into a corner of the choir, with the devout intention of praying to God and St. Francis for the soul of the departed Brother, his companion. And as he persevered with prayers and tears in his supplications till midday, when all the others had gone to sleep, he suddenly heard a great noise in the cloister. At which he turned his eyes in affright towards the sepulchre of his Brother: and he saw, standing in the entrance to the choir, St. Francis, and behind him, a great multitude of Brothers, around the sepulcher. Looking further, he saw in the midst of the cloisters a great fire, and in the midst of the flames thereof the soul of his departed companion. And looking back again, he saw Jesus Christ walking within the cloisters, with a great multitude of angels and saints.

He beheld these things in great amazement, and he saw that when Christ passed in front of the choir, St. Francis with all his Brothers knelt down, and said thus: "I pray thee, my dearest Lord and Father, by that inestimable charity Thou didst show to the human race in Thine incarnation that Thou wouldst have mercy on the soul of my Brother, that burns in yonder flame;" and Christ answered nothing, but passed on. And as He returned a second time, and passed in front of the choir, St. Francis knelt again with his Brothers, as at the first time, and prayed again in this manner: "I pray Thee, most compassionate Father and Lord, by the immeasurable charity which Thou didst show to the generations of men when Thou didst die on the wood of the Cross, that Thou wouldst have mercy on the soul of my Brother." And again Christ passed as before, as though He heard him not. And as he went round the cloisters, He returned a third time, and passed in front of the choir, and then St. Francis kneeling, as at the first, showed Him his hands and his feet and his breast, and said: "I pray Thee, most compassionate Father and Lord, by the great pains and great consolation which I sustained when Thou didst impress these Stigmata on my flesh, that Thou wouldst have mercy on the soul of my Brother that is in this fire of purgatory." O wonder! as St. Francis thus besought Christ the third time, and prayed for the sake of his Stigmata to be heard, immediately He stood still, and looking on the Stigmata, He said: "Francis, to thee I concede the soul of thy Brother." And by this, He certainly wished to honor and confirm the glorious Stigmata of St. Francis, and evidently to testify that the souls of his Brothers who enter purgatory can by no means more quickly be delivered from their pains, and conducted into the glories of paradise, than by virtue of those Stigmata, according to the words which Christ spoke to St. Francis when He imprinted them upon him. For as soon as He had spoken these words, the fire disappeared from the cloisters, and the soul of him that was dead came to St. Francis, and together with him, and with Christ, and with all that blessed company, following their glorious King, went up into heaven. At which his Brother, who had prayed for him, seeing him freed from his pains, and conducted to paradise, was filled with the greatest joy, and went and told the other Brothers all the vision as it had befallen him: and they, with him, praised and returned thanks to God.

HOW a noble knight devoted to St. Francis was assured of his death, and of the sacred Stigmata.

A NOBLE Knight of Massa di San Pietro, named Landolfo, who was specially devoted to St. Francis, and had received from him the habit of the Third Order, was assured of the death of the Saint, and of the truth of the most sacred and glorious Stigmata in the following manner. When St. Francis was near to death, the devil entered into a certain woman who lived in the Castle of Landolfo, and cruelly tormented her, causing her to speak with so much subtlety, that she vanquished all the scholars and men of letters who came to dispute with her. And it came to pass that the devil left her free for two days, and returned on the third, to afflict her more cruelly than at first. Then Landolfo, hearing of this, went to the woman, and questioned the foul spirit that dwelt in her, as to the reason why he had thus departed for two days, and returned on the third, to torment her more vigorously than before. And the demon answered: "When I left her, it was because I, with all my companions who are in these parts, assembled together, and went in great force to the death of the beggar, Francis, to dispute with him, and to take his soul; but being surrounded and defended by a greater multitude of angels, and carried by them straight into heaven, we returned in confusion; wherefore I returned and rendered to this miserable woman that which I had left undone for two days."

Then Landolfo abjured him, in the Name of God, to tell the truth as to the sanctity of St. Francis, whom he affirmed to be dead, and of St. Clare, who was living. And the demon replied: "Whether I will or no, I must speak that which is the truth. God the Eternal Father was so incensed against the sins of the world, that it appears He would, within a little time, have pronounced the final sentence against the men and women in it, and have exterminated them, unless they repented. But Christ His Son, praying for the sinners, promised to renew His own life and His Passion in a man, namely, in Francis, the poor little beggar; by whose life and doctrine many should be brought back to the way of truth, and many also to do penance. And lo! in order to show the world that which He had done in St. Francis, He willed that the Stigmata and signs of His Passion, which He had impressed upon his body during his life, should be seen and touched by many after his death. Likewise also, the Mother of Christ promised to renew her virginal purity and humility in a woman, namely, in Sister Clare, insomuch that she should reclaim many thousands of women from our hands. And thus God the Father, being appeased by these promises, suspended His final sentence."

Then Landolfo, wishing to know for certain whether the devil, who is the source and the father of lies, had spoken the truth in this matter, and especially as to the death of St. Francis, sent one of his trusted attendants to Assisi, to St. Mary of the Angels, to know whether St. Francis were living or dead. When the said attendant arrived, he found it so of a truth, and returning to his lord, told him that precisely at the day and hour that the devil had said, St. Francis had passed away from this life.

HOW Pope Gregory IX, having doubted of the Stigmata, was enlightened concerning them.

LEAVING aside all the miracles which are recorded of the most holy Stigmata of St. Francis, and which are to be read in his Legend, it remains to relate in conclusion of this fifth consideration, how Pope Gregory IX, doubting somewhat of the wound in the side of St. Francis, as he himself afterwards related, saw St. Francis in a vision one night, lifting his right arm a little, and showing him the wound in his side. After which he asked for a phial, which being brought, St. Francis placed it under the wound; and it seemed to the Pope in very deed that it was filled to the brim, with blood mingled with water flowing from the wound; and from that hour, all doubt departed from him. And afterwards, with the counsel of all the Cardinals, he approved the sacred and holy Stigmata of St. Francis, and in consideration of them, granted to the Brothers special privileges by a Papal Bull, and this he did at Viterbo, in the eleventh year of his Pontificate; and also in the twelfth year, he granted still greater privileges. Furthermore, Pope Nicholas III and Pope Alexander granted copious privileges, according to which, anyone denying the most holy Stigmata of St. Francis, might be proceeded against as a heretic.

And here ends the fifth consideration on the sacred and glorious Stigmata of our Father St. Francis, whose life may God give us grace to follow in this world, that by the virtue of the same glorious Stigmata we may merit to be saved, and to be with him in paradise. To the praise of Jesus Christ, and of His poor little one St. Francis. Amen.

PART II

THE LIFE OF
BROTHER JUNIPER

THE LIFE OF
BROTHER JUNIPER

1

HOW Brother Juniper cut off the foot of a pig, to give to one who was sick.

ONE of the most chosen disciples and first companions of St. Francis was a certain Brother Juniper, a man of profound humility, of great fervor and charity, with regard to whom St. Francis said once, speaking with some of his saintly companions: "He would be a good Friar Minor who had conquered the world and himself like Brother Juniper."

It came to pass once, at St. Mary of the Angels, that, inflamed with the love of God, he went to visit a sick Brother, and with great compassion asked him: "Can I do you any service?" The patient replied: "It would be a great comfort to me if you could get me a pig's foot to eat." Immediately Brother Juniper said: "Leave it to me, you shall have it at once." Away he goes and snatches a knife from the kitchen, and runs in fervor of spirit to the wood, where a number of pigs were feeding, and having thrown himself upon one of them, cuts off its foot and flees, leaving the pig thus mutilated. He returns and washes and dresses and cooks the foot, and with much diligence having well prepared it, he bears it with great charity to the invalid; who ate it with avidity, to the great consolation and joy of Brother Juniper, whilst he in high spirits, to amuse the sick man, recounted his assault on the pig.

In the meantime, the keeper of the pigs, who had seen him cutting off the foot, went and told the whole affair in detail with great indignation to his master, who when he had heard it, came to the house of the Brothers, calling them hypocrites, thieves, liars, rascals, and good-for-nothings, and saying: "Why did you cut off my pig's foot?" At the great disturbance which he made, St. Francis came out with all the Brothers, and humbly excusing himself and them, as ignorant of what had happened, tried to pacify him by promising to compensate him to the last farthing. But for all this the man was not pacified, but went away in a rage, still uttering menaces and threats, and repeating over and over, how maliciously they had cut off the foot of his pig. And listening to neither excuse nor promise, he departed as angry as he came, leaving all the Brothers stupefied and amazed.

But St. Francis, full of prudence, thought it over and said in his heart: "Can Brother Juniper have done this through indiscreet zeal?" And he had Brother Juniper called to him secretly, and asked him, saying: "Did you cut off the foot of a pig in the wood?" And Brother Juniper, not as one who had committed a fault, but rather as one who had performed a great act of charity, answered him joyously: "It is true, sweet Father mine, that I cut off the foot of a pig, and for the reason, be pleased to listen, my Father, feelingly. I went out of charity to visit the sick Brother;" and then he told him in detail all he had done, and added: "I tell thee thus, that considering the consolation it brought our sick Brother, and the pleasure he took in it, if I had cut off the feet of a hundred pigs, as I did of that one, I am sure it would have been pleasing to God." To which St. Francis, in just anger and very great displeasure, replied: "O Brother Juniper, why hast thou caused such a great scandal? Not without reason does this man complain and rail so greatly against us: and perhaps at this moment he is in the town, spreading an accusation against us of such ill-doing and with very great cause. Wherefore I command thee by holy obedience to run after him and overtake him, and throw thyself at his feet and tell him thy fault, promising to make such satisfaction to him, as that he shall have nothing to complain of against us, for certainly this has been too great an excess."

Brother Juniper was astonished at these words; and full of wonder that anyone should be angered by such an act of charity, because it seemed to him that temporal goods were nothing at all, except in so far as they were charitably shared with one's neighbor, he answered: "Doubt not, my Father, that I will soon compensate the man, and make him content. And why should I be troubled, seeing that this pig, whose foot I cut off, belonged more to God than it did to him, and that I did it for so great a charity?" And with this, he ran off and overtook the man, who had by no means recovered his equanimity, but was still angry beyond measure; and he narrated to him how and why he cut off the foot of the pig; and this with as much fervor and exultation and joy as if he had done him a great service, for which he ought to be greatly rewarded.

The man, full of anger and beside himself with fury, gave Brother Juniper many bad names, calling him a fool and a madman, a robber and the worst of brigands. But Brother Juniper cared nothing for these insulting words, and marveled within himself, for he rejoiced in being abused; and thought he could not have well understood the man, because there seemed to him room rather for praise than for blame. So he told the story over again, and throwing himself on the man's neck, kissed and embraced him, and told him how he had done it solely out of charity, inviting and pressing him to do the same with the rest of the pig; and with so much affection, simplicity and humility, that the man came back to himself, and not without many tears fell on his knees; and acknowledged his own fault in speaking and acting so violently against the Brothers, and goes and catches the pig and kills it, and having cut it up and cooked it, he bears it with much devotion and with many tears to St. Mary of the Angels, and gives it to the holy Brothers to eat in compensation for the abuse he had given them.

Then St. Francis, considering the simplicity and patience under adversity of the said holy Brother Juniper, said to his companions, and the others who were present: "Would to God, my Brothers, that I had a whole forest of such Junipers!"

II

AN instance of the great power which Brother Juniper had over the demons.

INASMUCH as the demons could not endure the purity of Brother Juniper's innocence and the depth of his humility, the following instance took place, by which this was most clearly shown. A certain person who was possessed, suddenly threw himself out of the way he was going, and contrary to all his usual customs, fled hither and thither by devious paths for about seven miles. And when his relatives, who pursued him, with great grief, had overtaken and interrogated him, asking why he had fled with such precipitancy, he replied: "The reason is this; because that idiot Juniper was passing along the way, and I cannot endure his presence or his aspect, therefore I fled into the woods." And they certified themselves of the truth that it was even so; that Brother Juniper had passed by at the same hour, as the demon had said. Wherefore St. Francis, when they brought him the possessed that he might heal them, if the evil spirit did not immediately depart at his command, used to say: "If thou depart not forthwith from this creature of God, I will fetch hither against thee Brother Juniper!" and immediately the demons, fearing the presence of Brother Juniper and unable to sustain the virtue and humility of St. Francis, departed from them.

III

HOW Brother Juniper, at the instigation of the devil, was condemned to the gibbet.

ONCE on a time, the devil wishing to terrify Brother Juniper, and to give him vexation and tribulation, went to a most cruel tyrant, called Nicholas, who was then at war with the city of Viterbo, and said: "My Lord, guard well your castle, because presently there will come hither from Viterbo a notorious traitor to put you to death, and set fire to your castle. And you shall know the truth of this, by these signs: He is attired as a harmless beggar, his clothes all ragged and tattered, and his hood falling in shreds upon his shoulders;

and he carries with him an awl, with which he is to take your life, and a tinder box, with which he is to set fire to the castle; if you do not find all this true, make an example of me." Hearing this, Nicholas had great fear, because he that told him these things seemed to be a man of weight and character. And he commanded that the guard should be set with diligence, and that if any man answering to this description appeared, he should immediately be brought before him.

Soon after, Brother Juniper came by alone, for, on account of his great perfection, he had leave to go out and to come in as he pleased. He was met first by some evil youths, who began to deride and to make a fool of him. He was not at all disturbed at this, but rather invited them to mock him the more. And when he arrived at the castle gates, the guards — seeing him so ill-favored, with his clothing all torn and ragged, for he had given part of his habit away on the road to the poor, for the love of God, and had no appearance of a Friar Minor about him, and because the signs they were given to expect seemed manifest upon him — with great fury seized him, and led him before their master, the tyrant Nicholas. And having searched him for arms they found in his sleeve an awl, with which he used to mend his sandals; and a flint, which he carried in order to make a fire, when he remained, as he oftentimes did, in the woods and deserts.

Then Nicholas, seeing the signs which he was to expect, according to the testimony of the accusing devil, commanded that they should bind him with cords; and this was done with so much cruelty, that they entered even into his flesh. Then he had him put upon the rack, and his arms dragged back and dislocated, and all his body tortured without mercy. And being asked who he was he replied: "I am a very great sinner."

Then they asked him, further, if he had come to betray the castle, and give it up to the Viterbese; and he answered: "I am a great traitor, and unworthy of any mercy." And they asked him, if he had meant with that awl to take the life of their master, Nicholas, and to set fire to his castle; and he replied: "Much worse things would I do, if God permitted it." Then Nicholas, overcome with anger, stopped the examination, and without further ceremony, in hot haste condemned Brother Juniper, as a traitor and homicide, to be tied to the tail of a horse, and dragged along the ground to the gallows, and then to be hanged by the neck. And Brother Juniper made no defense, but as one who, for the love of God, contents himself in adversity, remained altogether joyful and at peace. But as they carried into execution the commands of their master, and tied him by the feet to the tail of a horse, and dragged him along the ground, he neither complained, nor bewailed himself, but like a gentle lamb led to the slaughter, so he went with all humility. And all the people ran together to this spectacle, to see such hasty justice and cruel vengeance executed on him; but no one recognized him.

Nevertheless, as God willed it, a good man, who had seen Brother Juniper captured and so hastily condemned, ran to the house of the Friars Minor, and said: "For the love of God, I beseech you come quickly, for an unfortunate man has just been seized, and on the instant sentenced, and led away to death: come without delay, that he may place his soul in safety in your hands, for he appears to me to be a good man, and no time has been given him to make his confession, but he is led already to the gallows, and seems neither to care for death, nor for the salvation of his soul; I entreat you to come quickly." The Guardian, who was a compassionate man, departed in haste to secure the man's salvation; but when he got there, the crowd of people who had come to see the execution was so great, that he could not push his way through. And as he waited and watched for the moment when he might do so, he heard a voice from amongst the people cry: "Stay, stay, wretches! you hurt my legs." At the sound of his voice the Guardian thought he recognized Brother Juniper; and throwing himself with all his might into the crowd, he got through, and removing the covering from his face, saw that it was in truth Brother Juniper; and in his compassion, he would have taken off his own habit, and clothed him with it; but Brother Juniper, with a cheerful countenance, and beginning to laugh, said: "O Guardian, you are too fat, it would look ill to see you naked; I will not have it."

Then the Guardian, with many tears, entreated the executioners and all the people to delay a little whilst he went and prayed the tyrant Nicholas to pardon him. And the executioners, thinking it was a relation of his and consenting to wait a few moments, the devoted and afflicted Guardian, weeping bitterly, went to Nicholas, and said: "My lord, I am in such grief and amazement that my tongue refuses to speak, for here in this territory is committed today the greatest sin and the greatest wrong that has ever been done, from the days of our fathers; and I believe it must have been done through ignorance." Nicholas heard him patiently, and said: "What is this great wrong and evil which is committed today in this territory?" The Guardian answered: "My lord, that you have condemned to a most cruel death, and I believe without any cause, one of the holiest Brothers in all the Order of St. Francis, to which you are singularly devoted." Then said

Nicholas: "Tell me then, Guardian, who is it? for perhaps without knowing it I have done a great wrong." The Guardian said to him: "He whom you have condemned to death is Brother Juniper, the companion of St. Francis."

Nicholas was stupefied at these tidings, for he had heard of the fame of Brother Juniper, and of his holy life; and pale with terror, he ran with the Guardian to where Brother Juniper was, and unbound him from the tail of the horse, and set him free; and before all the people he threw himself at his feet, and with many tears confessed his fault, in the injury and wickedness he had perpetrated against this holy Brother; and he added: "I believe, verily, that the end of my evil life draws near, since I have outraged this holy man without any cause; God will let my sinful life end in a few days hence by a dreadful death, although I did it in ignorance." And Brother Juniper pardoned him freely; nevertheless, God permitted that, a few days after, this tyrant Nicholas ended his life by a cruel death. And Brother Juniper departed, leaving all the people edified by what they had seen.

IV

HOW Brother Juniper gave to the poor, for the love of God, all that he had in his power to give.

SUCH pity and compassion had Brother Juniper for the poor, that whenever he saw anyone naked, or badly clothed, he immediately took off his tunic and the hood from his head, and gave it to them: wherefore the Guardian forbade him under obedience to give away the whole of his tunic, or any part of his habit, to anyone. It came to pass that a few days after he met a poor man half naked, who prayed Brother Juniper for an alms, for the love of God: to whom the Brother with much compunction replied: "I have nothing I could give thee, except my tunic; and I am bound under obedience by my Superior not to give that to anyone, or even a part of my habit; but if you pull it off my back, I shall not resist you."

He spoke not to the deaf; and forthwith the beggar pulled his tunic over his head, and went his way, leaving Brother Juniper naked. And when he returned home, they asked him where his tunic was; to which he replied: "A good man pulled it off my back, and went away with it." And this virtue of compassion still growing in him, he was no longer content with giving away his tunic, but gave also the mantles of the others, and the books and ornaments of the church, and all that he could lay his hands on, to the poor. And for this reason the Brothers left nothing open or lying about, because Brother Juniper gave everything away for the love of God, and to His praise.

V

HOW Brother Juniper detached some bells from the altar, and gave them away for the love of God.

Brother Juniper was one day at Assisi, deeply meditating before the altar of the convent; and it was near the time of the Nativity of our Lord. Now this altar was very richly decked and adorned; and the sacristan begged him to remain and watch by it, whilst he went away to get something to eat. And as he continued in devout meditation, a poor woman came and begged an alms for the love of God. Then said Brother Juniper: "Wait a little, and I will see whether I can get thee something from the ornaments of the altar." And there was on this altar a fringe of gold, richly worked, and with little silver bells of great value. And Brother Juniper said: "These bells are a superfluity"; and he took a knife, and cut off the whole of them, and gave them to the poor woman, out of compassion.

The sacristan had not eaten three or four mouthfuls before he began to bethink himself of Brother Juniper's ways, and to misdoubt greatly what might become of the ornaments of the altar, which he had left in his charge; he feared lest he should do some mischief out of the excess of his charity. And all in haste and in great suspicion, he rose from the table, and went back to the church, and looked to see if the ornaments of his altar were safe, and none missing; and there he saw the fringe cut up, and all the bells gone: at which he was greatly angered and scandalized. But Brother Juniper, seeing his perturbation, said: "Do not put yourself out about these bells, for I have given them to a poor woman, who was in the greatest need of them; and here they were of no use whatever, but a piece of vain and worldly pomp." Hearing this, the sacristan in much distress immediately ran through the church, and all over the city, seeking everywhere if perchance he might find them again; but he neither found them, nor any person who had seen anything of them. Wherefore, returning to the convent in a rage, he took up the fringe and carried it to the General who was then at Assisi, and said: "Father General, I crave justice against Brother Juniper, who has spoiled my fringe, the best there was in the sacristy; now see how he has cut it to pieces, and torn off all the silver bells, and says that he has given them away to a poor woman." The General answered: "Brother Juniper has not done this, but your own stupidity; for you ought to know at this time of day, his way of going on; and I tell you that I marvel he has not given away the whole thing, but all the same, I will correct him severely for this affair." And calling all the Brothers together in Chapter, he summoned Brother Juniper, and in the presence of all the community, rebuked him severely on account of the said silver bells; and so wrath was he, that he raised his voice until it became quite hoarse.

Brother Juniper cared little or almost nothing for his words, because he delighted in reproaches and in being well abused; but he began to think of a remedy for the hoarseness of the Father General; and having received his reproof, he went straight off to the city to beg flour and butter with which to make a hasty pudding. And when he had returned and made the pudding a good part of the night was past so he lighted a candle, and went with his pudding to the cell of the General, and knocked. The General opened the door, and seeing him there, with the lighted candle and the pudding in his hand, asked softly: "What is this?" Brother Juniper replied: "My Father, when you reproved me today for my faults, I noticed that your voice became hoarse — I think that it must have been through excess of fatigue; and therefore I considered how to find a remedy, and made this pudding for you; therefore I pray you eat it, for I assure you it will soften your chest and your throat." The General answered him: "What an hour is this to come and disturb people!" And Brother Juniper said: "See, it is made on purpose for you; I pray you eat it without more ado, for it will do you a great deal of good." But the General, angry at the lateness of the hour and his importunity, commanded him to be off, saying that at such an hour he had no desire to eat, and calling him names, as a rascal and good-for-nothing. Brother Juniper therefore, seeing that neither prayers, nor coaxing, would move him, said: "My Father, since you will not eat, and this pudding was made on purpose for you, do this much for me: hold the candle and I will eat it." Then the General, being a pious and devout man, and perceiving the simplicity and piety of Brother Juniper, and that all this was done by him out of pure devotion, said to him: "Well, see now, since thou wilt have it so, thou and I will eat it together." And together they ate the pudding with a fervent charity each for the other; and much more were they refreshed by each other's devotion, than they were by the bodily nourishment.

VI

HOW Brother Juniper kept silence for six months.

Brother JUNIPER resolved once to keep silence for six months in this wise. The first day, for the love of the Heavenly Father; the second day, for the love of Jesus Christ, His Son; the third, for the love of the Holy Spirit; the fourth day, out of reverence to the most holy Virgin Mary; and thus, in order, each day, for love of some saint, he observed the six months silence.

VII

HOW to resist the temptations of the flesh.

As BROTHER GILES, Brother Simon of Assisi, Brother Ruffino and Brother Juniper were together one day, talking of God, and the salvation of their souls, Brother Giles said to the others: "What do you do in temptations of the flesh?" Brother Simon replied: "I consider the vileness and iniquity of the sin, and from this conceive such a horror of it, that it makes me fly from it." Brother Ruffino said: "I throw myself down on the ground, and pray so fervently, invoking the clemency of God, and of the Mother of Jesus Christ, that of a sudden I feel myself liberated." Brother Juniper answered: "When I feel the tumult of the diabolical suggestions of the flesh coming on, I run at once, and close the door of my heart, and to secure it, the fortress of my heart, I occupy myself in holy meditations, and holy desires, so that when the carnal suggestion comes and knocks at the door, I answer as it were from within, 'Begone, for the house is full already and can hold no more guests'; and thus I let no evil thought enter; and this thwarts the enemy, so that he departs, not only from me, but from all the country round." Then Brother Giles answered and said: "Brother Juniper, I hold with thee, for the flesh is an enemy which cannot be resisted, except by flight; for the carnal appetite which is a traitor within, and the senses of the body assaulting us from without, are enemies too many and too powerful to be vanquished in any other way. And hence, he who would fight in another fashion, will not often gain the victory after the fatigues of the battle. Let us therefore fly from this vice and we shall be victorious."

HOW Brother Juniper abased himself and gave glory to God.

ONCE on a time, Brother Juniper, desiring to abase himself as much as possible, took off all but his breeches; and making a parcel of his habit, and his other clothes, put it on his head, and thus went into Viterbo, to the public square, exposed to the derision of all who beheld him. Seeing him thus, the children and youths, supposing him to be out of his mind, did him much despite, throwing quantities of dirt at his back, pelting him with stones, and pushing him hither and thither; and thus persecuted and derided, he remained there the greater part of the day; and then returned to the convent. And when the Brothers saw him in this plight, they were much incensed against him, chiefly because he had gone all through the city, with his bundle of clothes upon his head. And they reproved him sharply, making him many reproaches. And one said: "Lock him up"; another said: "Hang him"; and another said: "Nothing can be too bad for him, after giving such bad example, and exposing himself and the whole Order." And Brother Juniper, full of joy, answered: "Well and truly do you speak, for I am worthy of all these punishments, and even greater."

HOW Brother Juniper in order to abase himself played at seesaw.

AS BROTHER JUNIPER was going once to Rome, where the fame of his sanctity had already spread abroad, many of the Romans through their great devotion for him, went forth to meet him; and Brother Juniper, seeing so many people coming, planned in his mind how to turn their reverence into emptiness and absurdity. There were two children by the wayside, who were playing at seesaw, having placed one piece of wood across another, and each of them holding on by one end, they went up and down. Brother Juniper therefore took one of the children off the plank, and mounted himself, and so began to seesaw up and down with the other. In the meantime the people came up, and marveled to see Brother Juniper thus engaged. Nevertheless with great devotion they saluted him, and waited until he should have finished his game of seesaw, to accompany him with all honor to the convent. And Brother Juniper concerned himself but little with all their salutations, reverence, and waiting on him, but remained much absorbed in his balancing. And waiting thus a great while, some began to be annoyed, and to say: "How stupid this is!" Others, knowing his ways, only conceived a greater devotion for him; but all the same they all departed, and left Brother Juniper to his seesaw. And when they were all gone, Brother Juniper got down, quite consoled because he had seen that many held him for a fool. And he went on his way, and entered Rome in all meekness and humility, and so arrived at the convent of the Friars Minor.

X

HOW Brother Juniper once cooked a fortnight's dinner for the Brothers.

As BROTHER JUNIPER was once staying in a very small house belonging to the Friars, it happened that for some reason all the Brothers were obliged to go out, and only Brother Juniper remained in the house. Therefore the Guardian said: "Brother Juniper, all of us are going out, so see that, when we come home, you have cooked some small refreshment for the Brothers on their return." And Brother Juniper replied very willingly: "Leave it all to me." When all the others were gone, said Brother Juniper to himself: "What useless care and solicitude is this, that one Brother should be lost in the kitchen, and kept away from prayer? For a certainty, I am appointed to cook for this once: I will do so much at a time, that all the Brothers, and more, if more there were, shall have enough for a whole fortnight." So, full of business, he went off to the farm, and brought several large earthenware pots for cooking, and procured fresh and dried meat, fowls, eggs and herbs, also firewood in plenty, and lighting his fire, put all on to boil — fowls in their feathers, and eggs in their shells, and all the other things in the same fashion.

When the Brothers returned home, one of them, who was well aware of Brother Juniper's simplicity, went straight to the kitchen, and there found many and huge pots on a raging fire; and sat himself down, looking on with astonishment, and saying nothing but watching with what solicitude Brother Juniper attended to his cooking. Because the fire was very fierce, and that he could not well get near his pots to skim them, he took a plank, and tied it tightly in front of him with cords to his body, and thus jumping from one pot to another, made a delightful spectacle. After watching him for some time, to his great amusement, the other Brother went out of the kitchen, found the rest, and said to them: "I assure you that Brother Juniper is cooking for a wedding." The Brothers took his words for a joke; but Brother Juniper presently lifted his pots from the fire, and rang the bell for the repast. And as they went in to dinner, he entered the refectory, with all his dishes, his face crimsoned with fatigue and the heat of the fire; and said to them all: "Eat well, and then let us all go to prayer, and let none think of cooking any more for a while, for I have cooked dinner enough today to last for a fortnight." And he placed his stew, of which there was not a pig in all the Roman province famished enough to have eaten, on the table before the Brothers. But Brother Juniper praised up his cooking, to give them an appetite; and seeing that the Brothers ate nothing, he said: "Now such fowls as these are comforting food for the brain, and such a stew as this will strengthen your bodies, it is so good." And the Brothers remained lost in devout astonishment at Brother Juniper's piety and simplicity.

But the Guardian, annoyed at such stupidity, and so much waste of good food, reproved him with great severity. Then Brother Juniper all at once threw himself on the ground on his knees before the Guardian, and acknowledged his fault against him and against all the Brothers, saying: "I am the worst of men; such a one commits such a crime, and has his eyes put out for it; but I deserve it much more; another is hanged for his faults, but I am more deserving of it for my evil deeds, who am always wasting the good things of God and of the Order." And thus sorrowfully he went away, and would not appear before any of the Brothers all that day. But when he was gone, the Guardian said: "Well-beloved Brothers, I would that every day this Brother of ours spoilt as many good things as today if we had them, solely for our own edification; for out of his great simplicity and charity he has done it all."

XI

HOW Brother Juniper went to Assisi, once on a time, for his own confusion.

WHILST Brother Juniper was staying once in the valley of Spoleto, he heard of a great solemnity then going on at Assisi, at which a great number of people were assisting with much devotion, and the wish came to him to assist at it also. And behold, he stripped himself of all but his breeches, and thus he went his way, passing through Spoleto, and right through the middle of the city, and so arrived at the convent. The Brothers, much put out and scandalized at his appearance, rebuked him sharply, calling him foolish and imbecile, and reproaching him with bringing confusion on the whole Order of St. Francis and wanted to chain him up as a madman. And the General also, who was then at the convent, called him up before all the Brothers, and in the presence of the whole community, gave him a stern and severe reproof. And after many words of vigorous indignation, he said to him: "The nature of your fault is such, and so great, that I know not what penance to impose on you." Then said Brother Juniper, as one who delighted in his own confusion: "My Father, I will tell thee: let me, for penance, return to the place whence I came to this feast, in the same manner that I came here."

XII

HOW Brother Juniper was ravished in spirit during the celebration of the Mass.

As BROTHER JUNIPER was one day hearing Mass with much devotion, he was ravished, through the elevation of his mind, for a long time. And being left alone and far from the Brothers, as soon as he came to himself, he began thus to say, with great fervor: "O my Brothers, who is there in this world so exalted, that he would not willingly carry a basket of dung upon his back, if there were given him for it, a house full of gold? Alas, why are we unwilling to carry a little shame, in order that we may attain to the Blessed Life!"

XIII

OF the sadness which Brother Juniper felt at the death of his companion, Brother Amazialbene.

BROTHER JUNIPER had a companion whom he loved intimately, whose name was Amazialbene; one who possessed the virtue of patience and obedience in the highest degree, insomuch, that if he had been beaten all day long, he would neither have complained nor protested with a single word. He was often sent to Houses where the communities were ill-disposed in their conversation, in which he received much persecution, all of which he bore most patiently, without a word of complaint. According to the bidding of Brother Juniper, he wept or laughed. And at last he died, as it pleased God, in the best repute.

When Brother Juniper heard of his death, it gave him such sadness of mind, as never in his life he had suffered before through any exterior cause. And thus he showed with outward signs the great bitterness of soul within him saying, "Woe is me to whom now remains no good thing; and all the world is become distasteful to me through the death of my sweet and beloved Brother Amazialbene!" And he said, "If it were not that the Brothers would give me no peace afterwards I would go to his grave, and take up his head, and of the skull I would make two vessels, one of which I would always eat out of in his memory and in my devotion, and the other I would drink out of when athirst."

XIV

OF the hand which Brother Juniper saw in the air above him.

BROTHER JUNIPER being one day at his prayers, and perhaps, thinking of his good works, there appeared to him a hand up in the air, and with his bodily ears, he heard a voice, saying to him: "Brother Juniper, with that hand thou canst do nothing." At which he rose with haste, and lifting, and directing steadfastly his eyes to heaven, said with a loud voice running all the while through the Convent: "It is indeed true: it is indeed true." And this he continued to repeat for a considerable time.

XV

THE example of Brother Leo, when St. Francis commanded him to wash the stone.

As ST. FRANCIS was speaking with Brother Leo one day, on Mount Alvernia, he said to him: "Brother Little Sheep, wash this stone with water." And forthwith Brother Leo fetched water, and washed it. With great joy and delight, St. Francis said: "Wash it with wine"; and he did so. "Wash it," said St. Francis again, "with oil"; and this also was done. Then said St. Francis: "Brother Little Sheep, wash this stone with balsam," and Brother Leo replied: "O sweet Father, how should I have balsam in so wild a place as this?" And St. Francis said to him: "Know, Brother Little Sheep of Christ, that this is the stone on which Christ sat, when once He appeared to me here; and therefore I bade thee wash it four times without answering me, because Jesus Christ promised me four singular graces for my Order. The first is, that all who love my Order and the Brothers sincerely, shall have the grace of final perseverance, and by the Divine favor make a good end. The second, that all who persecute this Order shall be notably punished. The third is that no wicked man, persevering in his wickedness, shall be able to remain long in the Order. The fourth, that this Order shall continue until the judgment day."

PART III

THE LIFE OF
BROTHER GILES

THE LIFE OF
BROTHER GILES

I

HOW Brother Giles and three of his companions were received into the Order of the Friars Minor.

AS THE example of holy men is calculated to excite in the minds of the devout hearer a contempt for transitory joys, and to inspire him with the desire of eternal salvation: to the honor of God, and of His most revered Mother, holy Mary, and for the edification of all who hear me, I will speak concerning the operation of the Holy Spirit in our holy Brother Giles who, while still in the secular garb, touched by the Holy Spirit of God, began to reflect with himself how he might, in all his works, please God alone.

About this time, St. Francis appeared, as a new herald of God, to give the world an example of a saintly life, of holy penance and humility; and two years after his own conversion, he was joined by a man of admirable prudence, and very rich in worldly goods, called Bernard, and by another named Peter of Catania, both of whom were attracted by the example of St. Francis to observe evangelical poverty, to distribute all their temporal goods to the poor, for the love of God, and to take to themselves the glory of patience and of evangelical perfection, and the habit of the Friars Minor. And with great fervor they promised to observe the rule all the days of their life, and this they did with great perfection.

Eight days after their conversion, and the distribution of their goods to the poor, which Brothers Giles witnessed, being still in the secular garb, and which excited the admiration of all, the example of these noble cavaliers of Assisi, thus despoiling themselves, so inflamed him with Divine love, that the next day, being the Feast of St. George, in the year 1209, he went betimes in the morning, as one solicitous about his salvation, to the church of St. Gregory, which was close to the Convent of St. Clare. And when he had finished his prayers, having a great desire to see St. Francis, he went toward the lepers' hospital, where he was dwelling with Brother Bernard and Brother Peter hidden in a mean and humble cottage. And coming to where two roads met, and not knowing which to take, he directed his prayer to Christ, the best of guides, Who led him straight to the cottage.

And as he went, St. Francis came out of the wood, where he had been in prayer, and came to meet him, wondering wherefore he had come. Whereupon Giles threw himself on the ground, and, kneeling at his feet, humbly begged that he would receive him as one of his companions for the love of God. Then St. Francis looking upon him, and seeing his devout aspect, answered and said to him: "Most beloved brother, God has given thee a great grace. If the emperor came to Assisi, and desired to make one of the citizens a knight of his court, or private chamberlain, ought not such a one to rejoice greatly? How much more oughtest thou not to rejoice that God had elected thee for His knight and beloved servant, to observe the perfect Rule of the Holy Gospel? And therefore stand firm and constant in the vocation to which God hath called thee." And he took him by the hand, and raised him up, and led him into the aforesaid little house,

and called Brother Bernard, and said to him: "The Lord
has sent us here a good Brother, for whom we shall all rejoice
in the Lord; let us eat together in charity."

And having eaten that which they had in the hut, St.
Francis went with Giles to Assisi, to procure cloth to make the
habit for the new Brother. And on the way they met a poor
woman, who asked them for alms for the love of God, and
not knowing how to provide for the poor woman, St. Francis
turned to Brother Giles, and with an angelic face, said to him,
"For the love of God, dearest Brother, let us give this mantle
to the poor woman." And Brother Giles obeyed the holy
Father so joyfully, that it seemed to him he saw this alms
fly swiftly up to heaven, and in spirit he flew straight into
heaven with it, whence he felt within himself an unspeakable
joy and renewal of heart. St. Francis having procured the
cloth, and made the habit, received Brother Giles into the
Order, who became, in the contemplative life, one of the most
glorious Religious the world had ever seen.

Immediately after the reception of Brother Giles, St.
Francis went with him to the province of Ancona, singing
with him as they went, and magnifying and praising the Lord
of heaven and earth. And he said to Brother Giles: "Son,
our Order shall be like to the fisherman who casts his nets
into the water, and catches a multitude of fishes, and keeps
the larger ones leaving the small ones in the water." Brother
Giles marveled at this prophecy, because there were in the
Order as yet only three Brothers and St. Francis, and up to
this time St. Francis had not preached publicly, but only as
he went along the way admonished and reproved the people,
both men and women, saying to them with simplicity and
affection: "Love and fear God, and do worthy penance for

your sins." And Brother Giles said: "Do that which my spiritual Father says to you, because he speaks right well."

II

HOW Brother Giles went to St. James's in Galicia.

AFTER a time, by permission of St. Francis, Brother Giles went once to visit the church of St. James the Great, in Galicia; and during the whole journey only once did he take something to eat, on account of the great dearth which then prevailed in all that country. For once, as he went along asking alms, and finding no one to give him any charity, it chanced that in the evening he halted by a threshing floor, where there yet remained some unthreshed beans: these he gathered up and made his supper on them, and there he slept that night, because he willingly sojourned in places solitary and remote from men, that he might the better give himself to vigil and prayer. And he was so much refreshed by God in this supper, that he could not have thought it possible to receive such refection, had he eaten of divers dishes.

And as he went further on his way, he met on the road a beggar, who asked him for alms, for the love of God. And Brother Giles in his charity, having nothing but the habit he wore, cut the hood away from his old mantle, and gave it to the poor man, for the love of God; and thus for twenty days, he journeyed on without a hood. And as he returned through Lombardy, a man called to him, to whom he went readily enough, thinking to receive an alms of him; but as he stretched out his hand, the other placed in it a couple of dice, inviting him to play. And Brother Giles, replying humbly, "God forgive thee, son," went on his way. And thus he went through the world, receiving much contempt and taking it all peacefully.

III

OF the manner in which Brother Giles lived, when he went to the Holy Sepulchre.

BROTHER GILES went, with the permission of St. Francis, to visit the Holy Sepulchre of Christ, and got as far as the port of Brindisi, and there he was detained several days, because there was no ship ready. And he, wishing to live by his own toil, bought a pitcher, and filled it with water, and went about the town crying: "Who will have water?" And by his toil, he earned his bread, and what was necessary for the life of his body, for himself and his companion: and afterwards he crossed the sea, and visited the Holy Sepulchre, and the other holy places, with great devotion.

And on the way back, he was detained in the city of Ancona for several days; and because he was accustomed to live by the labor of his hands, he made baskets of rushes and sold them, not for money, but for bread for himself and his companion, and for the same hire he also carried the dead to the cemetery. And when this failed him, he returned to the table of Jesus Christ, begging alms from door to door: and thus, with much toil and poverty, went back to St. Mary of the Angels.

IV

HOW Brother Giles praised obedience more than prayer.

A CERTAIN Brother was one day praying in his cell, when his Guardian sent word to him that he should go and seek alms by obedience. Whereupon, he went immediately to Brother Giles, and said, "My Father, I was at prayer, and the Guardian has commanded me to go and seek for bread, but it seems to me better that I should remain at my prayers." But Brother Giles answered him: "My son, hast thou not yet known, or understood, what manner of thing prayer is? True prayer is to do the will of your Superior; and it is a sign of great pride in one who has placed his neck under the yoke of holy obedience, when for any reason whatever he infringes it, thinking thereby to act more perfectly. The Religious who is perfectly obedient is like a rider mounted on a powerful horse, through whose strength he will pass fearlessly along the road; and on the contrary, the disobedient, complaining, and unwilling Religious, is like one who should be mounted on a lean, infirm, and vicious horse, for through a little fatigue, he will drop behind, and be slain or taken by his enemies. I tell thee that if a man had so great devotion and elevation of mind as to converse with angels, and whilst he thus conversed, he should be called away by one set over him, he ought at once to leave the converse of the angels and obey his Superior."

V

HOW Brother Giles lived by the labor of his hands.

BROTHER GILES was for a time in a Convent in Rome, and according to his custom ever since he entered the Order, he would live only by his own bodily labor; and this was his manner of life. Early in the morning he heard Mass with much devotion; then he went into the wood, which was eight miles from the city of Rome, whence he would gather and carry on his back a faggot of wood, and this he sold for bread and other necessaries.

On one occasion, as he was returning with a load of wood, a woman asked to buy it; and having made their bargain for the price, he carried it to her house. The woman, notwithstanding the bargain agreed upon, seeing that he was a Friar, gave him more than she had promised. Then said Brother Giles: "Good woman, I desire not to be overcome by the vice of avarice; therefore I will have no greater price than the bargain I made with thee." And thereupon not only would he take no more than the price agreed upon, but he left the half of it, and departed; at which the woman was inspired with a great devotion towards him.

Brother Giles did all his work in the same spirit of scrupulous honesty. He assisted in shaking down the olives and gathering the grapes. One day, when he was in the market place, a man was inquiring for some one to beat down his walnuts, and asking another to do it at a certain price; but the other excused himself, on account of the length of the way, and because the walnut trees were very hard to climb.

Then said Brother Giles: "Friend, if thou give me a part of the nuts, I will go with thee to beat them." Having made this agreement, he went with the man, and first making the sign of the most holy Cross, with great fear he climbed the walnut tree, and began to beat. And when he had done beating, the share that fell to him was so large that he could not carry it in his lap. Wherefore, taking off his habit and tying together the sleeves and the hood, he made a sack of it; and his habit, thus full of nuts, he placed on his back, and carried it into Rome, where with great joy he gave all the nuts away to the poor for the love of God. When the sickle was put into the corn, Brother Giles went with the rest of the poor to glean the ears; and if any gave him a handful of grain, he said: "Brother, I have no granary where I could store it:" and for the most part he gave away the ears he gathered, for the love of God.

Rarely did Brother Giles assist in these labors during the whole of the day, because he made it his bargain to have sufficient time to say the canonical hours, and not to fail in making his meditations. On one occasion, he went to the fountain of St. Sixtus to draw water for the monks with whom he sojourned, and a man asked him for a drink. But Brother Giles answered: "And how shall I carry the vessel half emptied to the monks?" The other, much offended, gave him many bad words and hard names; and Brother Giles returned to the monks greatly grieved. Then, borrowing a large vessel, he went quickly back to the fountain for more water, and found the man, and said: "Friend, take and drink as much as thy soul desires, and be not angry, for to me it seemed unbecoming to carry a vessel half emptied to those holy monks." Then the man repenting, and constrained by the charity and humility of Brother Giles, acknowledged his fault, and from that hour held him in great veneration.

VI

HOW Brother Giles was miraculously aided in a great necessity.

WHILST Brother Giles was in Rome, staying at the house of a Cardinal, as the time of the great Lenten Fast drew near, finding he could not have that quiet of mind he desired, he said to the Cardinal: "My father, with your permission, for my greater peace, I would pass the Lent with my companion, in some solitary place." The Cardinal answered him: "Well, my dearest Brother, and whither would you go? The dearth in these parts is great, and you know the country but little; let it please you to remain in my palace, since to me it is a singular grace to provide you with all you need, for the love of God." Nevertheless, Brother Giles resolved to go. And he departed from Rome, and went to a high mountain, where formerly there was a castle, and where there still remained a deserted church dedicated to St. Laurence; and therein he took up his abode with his companion, and devoted himself to constant prayer and meditation. They were unknown, and therefore little reverence or charity was shown them, so that they suffered great privations; and in addition, there was a heavy fall of snow which lasted several days.

And as they could not go outside the church, and no one sent them anything to eat, they remained fasting for three days. Then Brother Giles, seeing he could neither work for their bread, nor go out to seek alms, said to his companion: "My dearest Brother, let us cry to our Lord with a loud voice, that His compassion may provide for us in this extreme necessity, for many monks, being in great need, have cried to God, and His Divine Providence has supplied their wants." Therefore after this example they betook themselves to prayer, entreating God with all their hearts that He would send them relief in their great necessity. Then God, Who is all pitiful, looked upon their faith and devotion, and the simplicity, and fervor which had led them thither. A man who was looking toward the church said within himself: "Perchance there may be some good soul in that church doing penance, and, on account of the continuance of the snow, without means of living, who may therefore die of want." And inspired by the Holy Spirit, he said: "Yes, I will go and see whether my thought is true or not." And he took bread, and a bottle of wine, and went forth; and with great difficulty he arrived at the church, where he found Brother Giles and his companion praying most fervently, and so emaciated with hunger, that they had more the appearance of dead men than of living. He had great compassion on them, and after refreshing and comforting them, returned and told his neighbors of the extremity in which he found the Brothers, and begged for the love of God that they would provide for them; whence many, after his example carried them bread and wine and other things they had need of, for the love of God: and they arranged among themselves to provide for all their necessities during the whole of the Lent. And Brother Giles, considering their charity and the great mercy of God, said to his companion: "Dearest Brother, only just now we prayed to God to provide for us in our need, and He hath heard us; therefore it is meet that we should give Him thanks and praise, and pray for those who have succored us with their alms, and for all Christian people." And for the great fervor and devotion they had, God gave to Brother Giles such grace, that many through his example gave up this evil world; and many others, who were not disposed for the Religious Life, did great penance for their sins within their own homes.

VII

HOW a holy man, whilst at his prayers, saw the soul of Brother Giles enter into life eternal.

A CERTAIN holy man, who was engaged in prayer when Brother Giles passed from this life, beheld his soul, with a great multitude of other souls, coming out of purgatory and ascending into heaven; and he saw Jesus Christ with a multitude of angels come forth to meet the soul of Brother Giles who with all the other souls ascended with sweetest melody into the glory of paradise.

VIII

HOW, by the merits of Brother Giles, the soul of the friend of a certain Friar Preacher was delivered from the pains of purgatory.

WHEN Brother Giles was taken sick, a few days before he died, a Dominican Friar was sick unto death also; and this Friar had a friend, a Friar like himself, who, seeing his death approaching, said to him: "My Brother, I would, if God would permit, that after thy death thou return and tell me in what state thou art." And the sick man promised to return if it were possible: and he died on the same day as Brother Giles.

And after his death he appeared to the other Friar Preacher, and said: "It was the will of God that I should keep my promise to thee." Then said the living Friar to the dead: "How is it with thee?" And the dead replied: "It is well, because I died on the day on which a holy Friar Minor, named Giles, passed from this life also, to whom, for his great sanctity, Jesus Christ granted that he should lead all the souls then in purgatory, among whom was I, in great torment, unto the glory of paradise; and by the merits of this holy Brother Giles I was set free." And having thus spoken, he immediately disappeared; and this other Friar revealed the vision to no one. But presently, he sickened also; and immediately feared that God had thus punished him, because he had not revealed the virtue and the glory of Brother Giles; he asked to see the Friars Minor, and there came to him five couples; and he called together the Friars Preachers with them, and with great earnestness revealed to them the aforesaid vision; and when they had diligently inquired, they found it was even as he said, that on one and the same day the two had passed together from this life.

IX

HOW God granted special graces to Brother Giles, and of the year of his death.

BROTHER BONAVENTURE of Bagnioreggio used to say of Brother Giles that God had granted special graces to him for all those who with devout minds recommended themselves to him in those things which concerned the salvation of their souls. He worked many miracles both in his life and after his death, even as it appears in the Legend; and passed from this life into the supernal glory, in the year of our Lord twelve hundred and fifty-two, on the Feast of St. George, and is buried at Perugia, in the Convent of the Friars Minor.